William Blake Trask

Some of the Descendants of Lewis and Ann Jones of Roxbury, Mass.

Through Their Son Josiah and Grandson James

William Blake Trask

Some of the Descendants of Lewis and Ann Jones of Roxbury, Mass.
Through Their Son Josiah and Grandson James

ISBN/EAN: 9783337210137

Printed in Europe, USA, Canada, Australia, Japan

Cover: Foto ©ninafisch / pixelio.de

More available books at **www.hansebooks.com**

SOME OF THE DESCENDANTS

OF

LEWIS AND ANN JONES

OF

ROXBURY, MASS.

THROUGH THEIR SON JOSIAH AND GRANDSON JAMES

COMPILED FOR THE FAMILY

BY

WILLIAM BLAKE TRASK

BOSTON

PRINTED FOR PRIVATE DISTRIBUTION

MDCCCLXXVIII

150 copies.

GUNN, BLISS & COMPANY,
PRINTERS,
31 HAWLEY STREET, BOSTON.

☞ THE compiler has the pleasure of informing the family that to the generosity and thoughtfulness of Mr. JOSIAH MOORE JONES and his brother FREDERICK, both of Boston, and to Mr. NAHUM JONES, of Warwick, Mass., they are indebted for this publication.

W. B. T.

BOSTON, April 15, 1878.

INTRODUCTION.

"A LIVELY desire of knowing and of recording our ancestors so generally prevails," says the historian Gibbon, "that it must depend on the influence of some common principle in the minds of men. * * * The satirist may laugh, the philosopher may preach, but Reason herself will respect the prejudices and habits which have been consecrated by the experience of mankind." These remarks, though written a century or more ago, are just as true and applicable as if penned at the present time. For, if a desire to know their progenitors was general then, it is increased and intensified now. Moreover, it is getting to be almost a reproach, if a man —whose situation and circumstances will admit of it— does not perseveringly pursue the details of his family history, going back to the earliest ancestor in this country, and, if possible, to a transatlantic origin, tracing down, step by step, each generation to himself. This innate principle of the mind seeks manifestation among savage and civilized peoples, ancient and modern. Sometimes, in result, it takes the form of tradition, sometimes, of record. Often, it has to be laboriously sought for, particle by particle, like gold or silver in the mine. In other cases, previous minds have worked and delved, and their descendants enter into their labors. In regard to the family before us, it would be highly interesting, if it were in our power, to go back to some Johns or Johnes —which was the original form of the name, and as it is now sometimes spelled—in England or Wales, who was a forefather of our Lewis Jones. It would please us, also, to follow Lewis and Ann to the New World, and note their companions on the voyage thither. Possibly the "Apostle Eliot" may have been one of the number. For it is reasonable to suppose that many of the early settlers of Roxbury came in 1631 with that noted minister and teacher. Perhaps, some of the scholars who received from him the rudiments of their education, when Eliot was an instructor of youth in his native land, accompanied him to these western shores. And if any new comers here subsequently appeared, who belonged to his school-band there, the words of congratulation extended

to them first, could have been no more simple and ex-
pressive, than were the last two words he is said to have
uttered,—though used in another and a higher sense,—
"Welcome joy."

No attempt has been made to eulogize in the genealogy before us. It may be considered by some, perhaps,
that there is too much leanness attending our recitals.
In reply, we might say, that the family, in general, as we
know them, are practical people. They are men and
women of acts and deeds, not of mere sentiment or pro-
fession. They have furnished respected officers in the
church, and patriotic soldiers and citizens in the state.
Some have been worthy commanders in the military
companies of their respective towns. They have pro-
duced good husbands, housewives, sons and daughters.

Says the Hon. Marshall P. Wilder, in his admirable an-
nual address of January 2, 1878, before the New England
Historic-Genealogical Society, of which he is the President, "Some may inquire, of what use is all this research
into the dead past, this poring over the musty records of
by-gone days, this everlasting labor to complete a good
family pedigree? We reply, they bring together long
forgotten or estranged relatives, warm up the hearts of

thousands more or less connected in the past, unfold the history and preserve the memory of thousands gone long ago to their last home, enkindle a desire to preserve the names and memories of those of the loved and lost, and last and not least, preserve the history and progress of our country, and especially the customs, and manners, and principles of our progenitors, from the days when they left the father-land for the shores of this New World."

The place of residence of Lewis Jones, in Watertown, after his removal from Roxbury, has been designated by Dr. Bond, as a "ten acre lot, N. W. corner of Belmont and Grove streets." It is now in the town of Belmont. This estate was sold by his eldest son Josiah, executor of his father's will, to Sargeant John Coolidge, bounded south with the country road leading from Cambridge to Sudbury, now Belmont street, west with Deacon Bright (not Dwight, as stated on page 10 of this work), north with Joseph Mason, and east with a highway. Witnessed by John Chadwick and John Nevinson. The last mentioned was of East Horsley, co. Surrey, son of Rev. Roger Nevinson, of Hambledon, of the same county. He embarked at London, about May, 1668, and came to America as attorney for his father.

Capt. Wm. Paynter, of Barbadoes, born in 1640, by will made at Charlestown, August 24th, 1666, appoints his *brother, John Nevinson,* overseer, and leaves bequests to "mother Ann Jones, of Bristol," and to "father Jones." On the 30th of March, 1681, John Nevinson, of Watertown, was appointed "Sheperd" in place of "Goodman Jones."

In the preparation of this genealogy we have been greatly aided by the valuable matter contained in Bond's *History of Watertown.* From these pages we have drawn freely. In a note the Doctor says,—"A sheet was printed in Boston, in 1834, entitled, 'History of the Jones Family,' accompanied by a genealogical tree, prepared by Mr. William H. Jones, Jr., from a manuscript written several years previously by Israel Jones, Esq., of Adams, Mass. From this sheet, only lately put into my hands, I have received valuable information respecting some of the branches of this family."

The manuscript of Nahum Jones, of Gerry, Mass., now Phillipston, compiled in 1806, which was placed in our hands by a member of the family, has been of service.

The Town and Church Records, and Land Book of Roxbury, the Town Records of Weston, and the old burying ground there, the Probate Records of Suffolk and Middlesex, and the Registry of Deeds in both counties, have been put in requisition, either for information or confirmation in compiling the pages of this book. Much also has been furnished by the immediate members of the family, who were interested in having their branches properly presented.

There are some discrepancies in dates, as is often the case, in relation to births in the families within mentioned. As Dr. Bond has been found so accurate on all points where we have had opportunities of comparison, we have usually taken the liberty to follow him in reference to these dates. The arrangement of names is simple, and the plan we think easily understood. There is a consecutive numbering running through the genealogy. The character thus, × before a figure, denotes that the name is carried forward to a paragraph corresponding to the figure given. For example, × 3. Josiah. His family is given in paragraph —— 3 ——, and so on. References are made, forward and back, as instance, this figure 3.

W. B. T.

Boston, April 15, 1878.

JONES FAMILY.

THE name of Jones is of Welsh origin. Next to the surname of Smith, in England, by a fair comparison in numbers, stands that of Jones. It is derived from John, which is also one of the most common of christian names. In a tabular list, we have seen, embracing many of the most prominent families in Scotland, John took the lead. The Registrar-general of England, some years ago, in one of his official reports, pleasantly remarked that "the name of John Jones is in Wales a perpetual incognito, and being proclaimed at the cross of a market-town would indicate no one in particular." Burke's General Armory describes seventy-three coats of arms of those bearing the name of Jones in England, Scotland, Ireland and Wales. It would tax, methinks, the logical or genealogical skill of a cute Old England or New England antiquary to decide to which, if either, of these three-and-seventy families thus armored, Lewis Jones and his tribe belonged. One coat of arms was granted as early as September, 1604; another to a Lord Mayor of London in 1620. Among the mottoes used on the various coats of arms are these: Cœlitus mihi vires; Deus pascit corvos; Esto sol testis; Frangas non flectes; Mors mihi lucrum; Marte et arte; Deus fortitudo mea; Integritate et fortitudine; Vince malum bono.* Others, taken literally: A pure conscience is a safeguard to its possessor; Till then thus; Look to the past. A motto in Welsh reads thus: Pawb–yn–ol–ei–arfer; in English, "Every one to his own custom."

The earliest ancestor of the family we purpose in these pages to follow, as has been hinted, was Lewis Jones,† who with his wife Ann or Anna, about the year 1640, joined the church in Roxbury, Mass. Their names are recorded in the hand writing of their pastor,

---

* A friend has kindly made a translation of the above mottoes, which we subjoin :—

1. I have strength from above. 2. God feeds the ravens. 3. Let the sun bear witness. 4. You may break but not bend. 5. Death is a gain to me. 6. By war and art. 7. God is my stay. 8. Through integrity and fortitude. 9. Overcome evil with good.

† The English records give us the name of another Lewis Jones—as we take it—who was about to embark for these western shores, in 1635. It is not probable

the Rev. John Eliot. Among the 64 donors to the Free
School in Roxbury, the last day of August, 1645, was
Lewis Jones, he agreeing, at that date, to pay the Feofees
of the school, 4 shillings, annually. We have been a little curious to ascertain the place of his abode in Roxbury. It seems to have been at what was called "the
Nookes," contiguous to Dorchester, not far from the
" Roxbury brook." As a matter of interest, on this
point, we have been able to furnish from an old book of
Records of the Town Lands of Roxbury, some of the
boundaries of the real estate of the first settlers, who
were neighbors to Lewis Jones. Before doing so, however, we will give a copy of the following entry in this
old book, as it is very difficult to decipher, and moreover, contains some facts in regard to the design of the
book, its date, and its purchase, which it may be well
to have in print.

---

that this passenger was the husband of Anna. The great disparity in their ages,—
if her grave-stone inscription and the entry on the record be correct,—would be
against a supposition of that kind, the tablet making her about thirteen years his
senior.

"13° DIE OCTOBRIS 1635.
ABOARD THE AMITIE GEORGE DOWNES MR BOUND TO ST. CHRISTOPHRS,
LEWES JONES [aged] 20."

See Drake's *Founders of New England,* page 111.

" The First day of the Fowerth Moneth Comonly
Called June 1639 this booke was bought by the Seaven
men then imployed in the Towne affaires for the entry-
ing of the Towne Lands and other Weighty bussinesses
being fully agreed upon W^ch may concerne the Inhabitants of this Towne of Rocksbury and payed for the
booke Fower shillings."

Among the land owners we introduce, for the purpose
above mentioned, John Gore, John Dane, Phillip Tory,
John Gorton, and Widdow Gardner.

JOHN GORE.—The lott of Edward White, by the lott
of John Gore, on the south, sold to widdow Morrick, &
by her to John Gore ; with a wood lott of tenn accres &
a halfe, lying betweene the lotts of Arthur Gary & *Lewis
Jounes*, in the Nookes. (Page 9.)

JOHN DANE.—And in the Nookes, next Dorchester,
late the land of Joseph Patching, being the third lott lying betweene William Chandlers heires & *Lewis Jones*
ten accres and a halfe. And bought of Thomas Beck-
with, being formerly the land of *Lewis Jones*, thirteene
accres & twenty rodds, lying in the Nookes, next Dorchester, being the south lott, lying betweene the land of
Joseph Patching & John Stone his assignes. (Page 60.)

PHILLIP TORY [now written Torrey], in the Nookes, next Dorchester, being the first lott, fiue acres & one quarter. And halfe an accre of salt marsh, more or lesse, lying in a Nooke neare Grauelly poynt, at the end of Thomas Halyes lott. (Page 61.)

JOHN GORTON. And in the last diuision in the Nookes, next Dorchester, being the ninth lott, lying between Gowin Anderson his assigns, & Phillip Meadows his assigns, thirteen accres and twenty rodds. And in the last diuision in the Nookes, next Dorchester, bought of Henry Farnham, five accres & one quarter, being the fift lott, lying betweene *Lewis Jones* & Edward Riggs. (Page 67.)

WIDDOW GARDNER, in the last diuision of the Nookes, next Dorchester, being the nineteenth lott, lying between John Stebbin & the assignes of John Matthews, seauen accres three quarters & twenty rodds. (Page 68.)

Having given some idea of the locality of Lewis Jones, in Roxbury, we now proceed to speak of his family and his removal. Of his four children, whose names have come down to us, Lydia was probably born in England, Josiah, it may have been, in Roxbury, Phebe, in the latter place, and Shubael, in Watertown. With his wife Ann, and two children Lydia and Josiah—Phebe having died in Roxbury—he went to Watertown, Mass., where he settled, it is presumed, about the year 1650.

On the 23d of April, 1679, Lewis Jones, of Watertown, planter, for 12 cords of wood, sold to Justinian Holden, of Cambridge, about 3 acres of land, bounded with the farm land of Holden, "and the great Fresh Pond surrounding the same."

Mrs. Ann Jones died before her husband, the following being a copy of the inscription on a stone in the ancient burying ground in Watertown, marking the place of her interment, as furnished by the late William Thaddeus Harris, LL.B., of Cambridge, in his "Epitaphs from the old Burying Ground in Watertown."

> Here Lyeth the Body of ANN
> JONES. Aged 78 years Dyed
> The 1 of May 1680
> Upon ye Death of y^t:
> Pious Matron
> She Lived a Pious Holy Godly Life
> Being Now Escaped Free From Hate & Strife.

Mr. Lewis Jones died in Watertown, April 11, 1684. His will was dated Jan. 7, 1678, and is as follows:

"In the Name of God, Amen. I, Lewis Jones, in Watertown, in New England, being at this p^rsent of p^rfect understanding & memory, though weak in body, comitting my soul into the hands of Almighty God, and my body to decent buryall, in hope of a Resurrection unto eternall life through the merrits and power of Jesus Christ my most gracious Savio^r and Redeemer ; do thus dispose of that estate which God hath gratiously given unto me : Considering the weak and help-less condition of my dear wife, Ann Jones, and of my son, Suball Jones, my will and pleasure is, that the whole of my Estate (after the discharge of my debts and my buriall) be improved for their supply, the benefitt of it, and also, the principal, if they stand in need there-of. And further, my will and pleasure is, y^t when the Lord shall please to remove either of them by death, that then that which re-maineth shall be wholly to the use of the other so long as either of them shall live ; & if the Lord shall so dispose that anything remain-eth after their death, that then what remaineth be divided, two parts to my daughter Lydia Whitney, if she be then living, & one to my son Josiah ; but if Lydia be dead, that then w^t remaineth be divided equally to my son Josiah, if living, or such of his children as shall be living, and the children of my daughter Lydiah that shall be then liv-ing, & of this my last will, I do constitute my son Josiah Jones, my sole Executo^r & do earnestly desire my loving friend and Brother John Stone to be overseer, to assist my son in the managing of y^e estate so as may be best for the comfort of my poor wife & child afores^d. And in confirmation hereof, I have set hereunto my mark and seale.

Simon Stone.   The marke $\mathcal{J}$ & seal of

John Stone.   LEWIS JONES,

this 7th of y^e 11th, 1678.

A Codicill annexed to y^e above s^d will, 19, 2, 1682 [after the death

of the wife of the testator]. As a further Addition to my last Will
and Testament, I do nominate & appoynt my assured friends, Simon
Stone & John Stone of Watertowne, to be Guardians unto my son
Suball Jones, to whose prudence and wisdom I do commit & send the
governm^t of my s^d son, & the disposall of all that Estate as well real
and p^{r}sonall to my s^d son bequeathed ; & I do hereby authorize & em-
power s^d Guardians or the Longest liver of them, to make sale of any
part of my house and lands as there shall appear to them needful for
the relief of my s^d son Suball Jones.

his mark.
LEWIS J JONES.

The above will was proved June 17, 1684.

JONATH. REMINGTON, Clericus.

An INVENTORY OF THE ESTATE OF LEWIS JONES, LATELY DECEASED,
OF GOODS & CHATTELL TAKEN BY US, WHOSE NAMES ARE
UNDER WRITTEN, THIS 20TH OF APRIL, 1684.

	£	s.	d.
The housing & land, . . .	035	00	00
A cow & a heifer, . . .	004	05	00
Wearing cloathes, ...	001	10	00
In ye ledging Room, one feather bed, two pillows, one bolster, one rug, three old blancketts, three sheets, curtans & bedstead, ...	05	00	00
One small flock bed, one coverlett, one bolster, two pillows, two sheets, one old straw bed, two blank- etts, & a Trundle bedstead, ...	002	04	00

One Chest, one Tablecloath, one napkin, with some
    other old linnen, one small box, one forme,   .   ooo 12 oo
In yᵉ fire Room, one brass kettle, two skillets, one
    old warming pan, ...   ooo 17 oo
Three small pewter dishes, one quart pot, more,
    some old pewter, ...   ooo 10 oo
Three iron potts & 2 pʳ of pot hooks, one frying pan,   oo1 10 oo
In books, ...   oo1 15 oo
One Tramell, one fire shovell, a pʳ of Tongs, one
    spitt, a pʳ of Bellows, with other small things,   .   oo 12 oo
Two Tables, one Chest, a kneading Trough, & 2
    old Chars, ...   ooo 16 oo
One halfe bushell, a baskitt, one pail,   .   .   .   ooo o6 oo
One beetle & wedges, one Ax, two pitchforks, wᵗʰ
    some old Iron & other lumber,   .   .   .   ooo 10 oo
In earthen ware, with two bags, ...   ooo o4 oo
Upon yᵉ chamber, one old fan, one old flock bols-
    ter, some old Cashe [*sic*] & lumber,   .   .   ooo 10 oo
In rye & malt, ...   ooo 18 oo
In barley, ...   ooo 14 oo
In Indian corne, ...   oo3 10 oo
In yᵉ cellar, one powdring Tub, four barrells, one
    old churne, one small Caske, two Earthen potts,
    & one keeler, & other lumber,   .   .   .   ooo 19 oo

     John Coolidge,   £o62 o2 oo
     John Bright,
     Munning Sawin.

Ap. 2, 1684, Josiah Jones, adm^r, took oath in Court hereto.

THO: DANFORTH, R.

Middlesex Probate Records, Lib. VI. *Fol.* 174.

Middlesex County Land Records, Book 9, *page* 168.

December 29, 1684. By deed of this date, Josiah Jones, executor of the last will and testament of his father, Lewis Jones, late of Watertown, deceased, John Stone, overseer to said will, and Simon Stone and John Stone, guardians to Suball Jones, as appeareth in the last will of the father of the said Josiah, for valuable consideration sell and convey to Sargeant John Coolidge, of said town of Watertown, dwelling house and orchard, and by estimation, ten acres of land (being estate of said deceased), bounded south with the country road, west with Deacon Dwight, north with Joseph Mason, and east with a highway.

Children of LEWIS and ANN JONES:

> 2. LYDIA,[2] born it is supposed in England ; married Oct. 30, 1656, Jonathan Whitney, who was born in England in 1634. He died, says Dr. Bond, in Sherborn, about 1702, where he resided as early as 1679. They had children : Lydia, Jonathan, Anna, John, Josiah, Elinor, James, Isaac, Joseph Abigail, Benjamin. See Bond's *Watertown*, p. 644.

✕3. JOSIAH,² b. probably in Roxbury, Mass., in 1643 ; d. in Weston, Oct. 3, 1714.

4. PHEBE,² b. in Roxbury, Jan. 21, 1645–6 ; d. July 6, 1650, "by a scald," says the church records.

5. SHUBAEL,² b. in Watertown, July 1, 1651. John and Simon Stone were on the 7ᵗʰ of Oct., 1684, appointed by the Court, guardians to said Shubael, he being afflicted, probably by some weakness or infirmity. Provision was made for him, as will be noticed, in his father's will.

—— 3 ——

JOSIAH² (*Lewis¹*), son of Lewis and Ann Jones, was born, it is supposed, in Roxbury, Mass., about the year 1643, for by two testimonies given by him in 1669, he describes himself as then about twenty-six years of age. He married Oct. 2, 1667, Lydia Treadway, daugher of Nathaniel and Sufferana (How) Treadway, of Watertown. Mr. Jones was a selectman in Watertown during the years 1685, '86, '87, '90, 1702, '09 ; was admitted a freeman, April 18, 1690 ; was a captain, one of the original members, and one of the first deacons of Weston church, to which office he was elected Jan. 4, 1709-10.*

---

* On the 9th of January, 1695, the inhabitants of the western precinct of Watertown, now Weston, agreed to build a meeting house. The spot selected was a little in front of the present house. The next year, agents were chosen to make a contract with the workmen to build what was appropriately called *The Farmers' Meeting House.* It was not finished, however, so as to be ready for use, till March,

About 1690 the three portions of Watertown (Watertown, Waltham and Weston), were designated as the precincts of Capt. Bond's company, of Capt. Garfield's company, and of Lieut. Jones's company.

Feb. 20, 1665-6, he purchased of John Stone and wife Sarah, of Watertown, a farm of 124 acres, on the north side of Sudbury highway, about two miles from said Sudbury, which his father, Simon Stone, purchased May 18, 1657, of Richard Browne, late of Watertown, deceased. (Middlesex Deeds. Lib. iv. fol. 217.) ·

On the 21st of April, 1684, he sold to John Bright, for £60, his share,—which was one-quarter—of the mills on Stony Brook, with 30 acres of land, bought of Nathan-

---

1700. They had no settled minister till Nov. 2, 1709, about eleven years and a half after the *Farms* had become a distinct precinct, when a church was gathered, and Mr. William Williams, of Hatfield, was ordained their pastor. The church consisted, at first, of eighteen male members, nine from other churches, and nine who had not been communicants. The latter were Josiah Jones, Thomas Weight, Joseph Allen, Josiah Jones, jun., Joseph Livermore, Joseph Allen, jun., Samuel Seaverns, Joseph Woodson and George Robinson. Jan. 4, 1710, two deacons were chosen, viz: Capt. Josiah Jones and John Parkhurst, who accepted the trust.

The exact date of the incorporation of the town, which was subsequent to the formation of the church, was given by Mr. Williams, their minister, who made an entry in the book of church records, in these words, "A brief and true record of the ecclesiastical affairs of the church, in the west part of Watertown, commonly called *Watertown Farms*—made a distinct town Jan. 1, 1712-13, and called *Weston.*" The first town meeting was called to be holden, March 2, 1712-13.

Compiled from Rev. Dr. Kendal's *Century Sermon,* delived at Weston, Jan. 12, 1813.

iel Treadway, Feb. 19, 1678-9, land bought of John Chadwick, with the house, &c., thereon. (Middlesex Deeds, Lib. ix. fol. 336.)

In the old cemetery at Weston, Mass., is a grave-stone, bearing the following inscription :—

> Here Lyes buried
> The Body of Capt.
> JOSIAH JONES,
> Who Deceased Octobr
> the 9th, 1714, in the
> 74th year of his Age.

It will be seen that there is a variance of three or four years between the inscription above and the two depositions below. The latter were copied verbatim from the originals on file in the Court House at East Cambridge.* The first of these testimonies bears the endorsement of Thomas Danforth.

Lydia, the widow of Capt. Josiah Jones, died at Weston. The inscription on her grave-stone reads thus :—MRS. LYDIA JONES, relict of

---

* Josiah Jones test. sworne in Court 6, 2, 1669.

> T. D., R. [Thomas Danforth, Register.]

The testimony of Josyah Jones, aged 26 years or theare abught, Do testyfy to this honered Corvtt that the thvrs day nyght before that John lyuermors house was broken vpe that the prisner Drake did ly in my lott, and that I did make after him to sudbvry but Cold not overtake him, and furder, all so, I do testyfy, that I saw a hole broken in to his leane to, whare a man might Creepe in and from that hole, I did see a mans pooking in to his dwelling howse, and ther I sawe the Cheast and boxe had bene opened, and that the lords day forlding be fore, I saw him trafilling with a white bage att his back, and my selefe and another did persew him three mills to see what he had in it, and then he came in the rode way, Right from John

Capt. Josiah Jones, who was ye first Deacon of ye Church in this Town, died Sept. 17, 1743, aged 95. So that she was born about 1648. In the Scotch Magazine, printed in Edinburgh in Scotland in 1743, the date of her death is given as Sept. 22. It further states, that "she lived to see her children, grand children, great grand children and their children, in all 296, of whom 233 remain alive." ["Nahum Jones's Register of his Ancestors and their Descendants. Much information contained in this Register was given me by my Grandfather (on my Mother's side), Capt. Aaron Jones, of Templeton, who is in his 84th year. Gerry, July 1, 1806." This manuscript of about 20 pages is before me. W. B. T.] Nahum, above, was Nahum^6, (No. 46), the school teacher.

Children of JOSIAH and LYDIA (Treadway) JONES.

6. LYDIA,³ b. Aug. 25, 1668; m. Jan. 2, 1687-8, Nathaniel Coolidge, Jr. (b. May 9, 1660), the son of Nathaniel and Mary (Bright) Coolidge. He settled in Watertown Farms, now Weston, and his name is the first on the list of the

---

lywermors house, and when we had ower taken him, we asked him what was his name, and he towld vs that his name was thomas skillkins, and furder sayth not.

Josiah Joanes, being about twenty six yerse of age, testyfieth and sayeth, that the goods wch ware tacen by warant by the Constiple of conkerd and Claimed by Samuel morse are the sayed Samuells goods, acording to what mark or discriptions he gaue of them befor ye constiple and my selfe, this being befor he saw ane of the goods.

Further sayith not.

Taken upon oath the seauenth day of April 1669.
Before me, Daniel Gookin.

original members of the Weston church. They had 6 children, Samuel, Lydia, Josiah, Mary, Abigail, Thankful. His wife, Lydia, died May 21, 1718. Mr. Coolidge died in Weston, Jan. 29, 1732-3.

7. JOSIAH,[3] b. Oct. 20, 1670 ; m. Abigail Barnes. He was elected deacon of the Weston church, Feb. 13, 1714-15, as successor of his father, but declined. He was a Lieutenant under his father, and then promoted to a Captain. He died Dec. 21, 1734. Abigail, his widow, died in Stockbridge, Nov. 4, 1749. They had 5 children, Daniel, Abigail, *Josiah*, William, Elisha. The latter was a Colonel, and Justice of the Peace. The fac-similes that follow are from Bond's History of Watertown, pages 312, 315. The first is that of the signature of the above Josiah Jones, who m. Abigail Barnes ; and the second, his son, Josiah, b. Oct. 24, 1701, who m. 1st Dec. 24, 1724, Anna Brown, dau. of Deacon Benjamin and Anna (Garfield) Brown, of Weston, and second, widow Sarah (Stoddard) Whittlesey.

Josiah Jones   *Josiah Jones*

8. MARY,[3] b. Dec. 10, 1672 ; m. July 3, 1693, Lieut. John Brewer, of Sudbury. He was born in 1669. eldest son of John Brewer, of Sudbury; resided at first in Sudbury, afterwards he settled in Watertown Farms (Weston). He died May 5, 1709, leaving widow Mary. Inventory, £533. 5. 6., including farm and 216 acres of other lands,

saw mill and grist mill. His widow was licensed Jan. 1,
1716-17, to keep a public house. They had 6 children,
John, Mary, Josiah, Daniel, William, Submit.

9. NATHANIEL,[3] b. Dec. 31, 1674. By wife Mary, he had 6
children, born in Weston, then moved to Worcester,
where he had 5 other children by the first wife. She died
and he married 2d ———— Flagg, and had 3 other children. Before the birth of the youngest (Jabez), he moved
to Falmouth, Maine. He was a Captain. Mr. Jones
died in Nov., 1745. By his two wives he had 14 children,
Phinehas, Nathaniel, (Daniel, 3d son of Nathaniel, was
killed in an attack on the French lines at Ticonderoga, in
1758,) Stephen, Noah, Jonas, Ichabod, Isaac, Sarah,
Mary, Eunice & Lucy (twins), Moses, Lydia, Jabez. We
shall have more to say, presently, of Stephen, the third
son, who married, in 1735, his cousin Lydia Jones, daughter of Capt. James Jones, his father's brother. Ichabod,
the sixth son and child of Nathaniel[3], above, bap. May
26, 1717, m. May 8, 1746, Apphia Coffin, of Newbury,
(b. in N., April 13, 1724, dau. of John and Judith (Green-
leaf) Coffin.) He settled in Boston, was a shipmaster ;
left one son, Hon. John Coffin Jones, who graduated at
Harvard College in 1768 ; a merchant of Boston, d. Oct.
25, 1829, aged 79. Jabez inherited his father's farm ;
was living at the age of 85 ; had three wives, and sons and
daughters. Nathaniel[3] was a selectman of Worcester,
1722 and 1723, and a representative in 1727.

10. SAMUEL,³ b. July 9, 1677, m. May 19, 1706, Mary Woolson
(b. Nov. 28, 1673), fourth child of Thomas and Sarah
(Hyde) Woolson, of Weston. He died in January, 1717-
18. The Town Records have it Jan. 25, Dr. Bond the
17th. His will, dated Jan. 14, 1717-18, was proved April
9th, 1718. His widow m. Oct. 1, 1724, Major Francis
Fulham, Esq., of Weston. He was from Marlboro'.
Samuel and Mary (Woolson) Jones had 3 children, Samuel, Moses, Mary.

✕11. JAMES,³ b. Sept. 4, 1679, d. Sept. 14, 1770.

12. SARAH,³ b. Feb. 6, 1681, m. May 20, 1704, John Warren (b.
March 15, 1684-5), eldest son and child of Ensign John
and Mary (Brown) Warren. Sarah (Jones) Warren died
in childbed, July 9, 1705, leaving Sarah, b. June 25, 1705.
Mr. Warren m. (2d) June 2, 1708, Abigail Livermore (b.
Oct. 9, 1683), daughter of Samuel and Anna (Bridge) Liv-
ermore. She died of dysentery, Oct. 31, 1743, aged 60,
and he m. (3d) June 20, 1744, widow Lydia Bond *née*
Spring, of Watertown. Her former husband was Thomas
Bond, who died May 17, 1737. Mr. Warren was chosen
Deacon of the Weston church in 1733.

13. ANNA,³ b. June 28, 1684, m. Dea. Joseph Mixer (b. Aug. 9,
1674), son of Isaac and Rebecca (Garfield) Mixer. He
died Dec. 10, 1723. Anna, his widow, died in 1736.
They had 9 children, Rebecca, Joseph, Sarah, Lydia, David, Mary, Josiah, Anna, Abigail.

14. JOHN,³ b. March 19, 1686-7, a carpenter, of Weston, m.

Dec. 8, 1715, Mehitable Garfield (b. Dec. 7, 1687), dau.
of Capt. Benjamin and Elizabeth (Bridge) Garfield, of
Watertown. Mr. Jones, Sept. 8, 1710, purchased of John
Holden and wife Grace, 27 acres and 60 rods of land,
part of the farm sold by Rev. James Sherman, of Sudbury, to Holden and John Traine.

John and Mehitable (Garfield) Jones had 9 children,
John, Eunice, Joseph & Benjamin (twins), Anne, Abra-
ham, Ezra, Abijah, Beulah. John, the father, died at
Weston, aged 82.

15. Isaac,[3] bap. May 25, 1690 ; bought a farm in Bolton, Conn.,
married and had a large number of children who lived to
mature age ; one account says 15 children, all of whom
lived till the youngest was 15 years old.

—— 11 ——

JAMES,[3] (*Josiah,[2] Lewis,[1]*) son of Josiah and Lydia (Treadway)
Jones, of Weston, was born Sept. 4, 1679. He m. Sarah
Moore, dau. of Capt. Moore, of East Sudbury. She had
several brothers, viz : Richard, who lived 90 years ; Nathaniel, 90 ; John, 90 ; Daniel, 85 ; Samuel, 80 ; James,
65 ; Jonathan, 40. (Manuscript of Nahum Jones, before
referred to.) He was one of the original proprietors of
Narragansett, Number 6, now Templeton, Mass. Capt.
James Jones died, according to the inscription on the
grave-stone, at Weston, Sept. 15th, 1770, aged 90.

On the same stone, we think, is the inscription to Sarah, his relict, who died Sept. 28, 1774, aged 90. These lines are beneath :

> Down to the Dead all must Descend,
> The Saints of God must Die ;
> While Angels Guard their Souls to Rest,
> In Dust their Bodies Lie.

The following is a copy of the Will of Capt. James Jones, of Weston, from the original on file at East Cambridge, co. Middlesex.

WILL OF JAMES JONES,[3] GRANDSON OF LEWIS.[1]

In the Name of God, Amen. I, James Jones, of Weston, in the County of Middlesex and Province of the Massachusetts Bay in New England, Gent", being infirm in Body, but of Sound disposing mind, mindfull of my Frailty, do make and Ordain This my last Will and Testament ; Firstly, Comitting my Soul to God Thro' our Lord Jesus Christ ; And my Body to be decently buried at the Discretion of my Executors hereafter Named. And as to the Temporall Estate Which God has given me I dispose off in Manner following.

Impr⁵. My Will is that my Debts and Funeral Charges be paid by my Executors hereafter Named.

Item. I give to my well beloved Wife all my Houshold Goods Within Doors (Except money and What is due to me in Money) and Also one Third part of my live Stock, to be for her Own Use and disposal. And Also one Third part of the Improvements of my real Estate, or the Income of it, and a Third part of the Buildings, Houses and Barns &c., during the time she remains my Widow.

Item. I give to my Eldest son James Jones, in Addition to What he has already recieved in Lands, The Sum of Twenty Shillings Lawfull money, To be paid in one year after my Decease, in full of his portion.

Item. I give unto my Grandchildren ; viz. Elijah, Isaac, Sarah, Solomon, Katherine, Hannah, and Samuel Robinson, The Children of my Daughter Sarah Robinson, Deceased, The Sum of Forty Shillings, Each, To be paid to Them as They Severally Come of Eage, viz, the Boys at the Eage of Twenty one years and the Girls at Eighteen or at Their Marriage, Which is in full of Their portion.

Item. I give unto my Daughter Lydia Graves (besides What she has rec^d), the Sum of Twenty Shillings, to be paid in one year after my Decease, in full of her portion. I also give to her four Children, viz, Stephen Jones, and Micah Jones, Five pounds Each, to be paid to Each of Them When They Come to the Eage of Twenty one years ; and To Rebecca Jones and Abigail Jones, Five pounds, Each, to be paid When They Come to the Eage of Eighteen years or at Their Marriage.

Item. I give unto my Son Ephraim Jones, the Sum of Twenty Seven pounds to be paid in one year after my Decease. Which Sum Together with what he has already recieved is in full of his portion.

Item. I give unto my daughter Elisabeth Baldwin, the Sum of Fourteen pounds, To be paid in one year after my Decease. Which is in full of her portion.

Item. I give Unto my Daughter, Mary Flagg, the Sum of fourteen pounds, To be paid in one year After my Decease. Which is in full of her portion.

Item. I give unto my Daughter Abigail Sanderson, the Sum of Fourteen pounds, to be paid in one year after my Decease, in full of her portion.

Item. I give unto my Daughter Katherine Davis, The sum of Fourteen pounds, to be paid in one Year after my Decease. Which is in full of her portion.

Item. I give and bequeath unto my two grandchildren, Solomon Jones and Sarah Jones (Children of my Eldest Son James Jones), the Sum of Seven pounds to Each of Them, to be paid to Solomon When he Comes to yᵉ Eage of Twenty one years, and to Sarah at yᵉ Eage of Eighteen or Marriage.

Item. I give unto my son Aaron Jones, one Moiety of my Mansion House and Barn and Homestall adjoining to yᵉ Moiety I have already granted to him by a Deed bearing Date October 19ᵗʰ, A.D. 1753, and also one Moiety of all the Other Lands Mentioned in yᵉ said Deed, and also I give unto my said son, one Moiety of my meadow land in the great Meadow Near the Meeting house ; and one Moiety of Several Lots of Land in Weston, Lying near Nathaniel Dewings, formerly Called Lands of Contention, and also one Moiety of My Lands lying in yᵉ Township of Paquoiagg.* I also give unto my said

---

* *Pequoiag*, now Athol, Mass., was incorporated as a town March 6, 1762. There are various ways of spelling this Indian name. We have two examples in the above will. It has also been written Paquoag, Payguage, Payquage, Payquaog, Perquage, Pequiog, Peyquage, Poquaig, Poquioug, Poquoiag, etc. Mrs. Rowlandson wrote it Bayquage. Originally the town of Athol was six miles square.

son, a Lott of Land in the Narragansett Township, No. 6, Which Lott as Drawn is No. 5.   Together With all the after Draught, & Divisions, to him, his heirs and Assigns forever, With all the rights, privileges & appurtenances Thereto belonging : he being Joyntly Obliged Together With my Son, Isaac Jones, hereafter Named, to pay the Legacy[s] and my Debts and Funeral Charges, &c.   I also give to him one Moiety of my Stock & Moveables Not before Willed.

Item.   I give unto My Other Son, Isaac Jones, one Moiety of y[e] Mansion House Wherein he Now Dwells, and of the Barn & Home-stall adjoining to the Moiety I have already granted to him by a Deed bearing Date October 19th, 1753, and also one Moiety of all y[e] Other Lands Mentioned in the said Deed.   I also give unto my said Son y[e] Other Moiety of my Meadow Near y[e] Meeting House, and of the several Lots of Land lying near Nath[l]. Dewings, and of My Lands lying in the Township of Paquiogg : having before Willed y[e] Other Moiety to my son Aaron.   I also give to my said son Isaac, a Lott of Land in y[e] Narraganset Township No. 6.   Which Lott as Drawn is No. 99, Together With all y[e] after Draughts and Divisions to him his heirs and Assigns forever, With all the rights priviledges and appurte-

---

Subsequently a portion was set off to Gerry, now Phillipston, afterwards another part to Orange, and still another to Royalston.   A portion of the town of New Salem, called Podunk (the Indian name of the locality), has been annexed to Athol.

See Appendix to Clarke's Centennial Discourse, delivered at Athol, September 9, 1850, at the celebration of the one hundreth anniversary of the organization of the church.

Rev. Elias Nason, in his *Gazetteer of Massachusetts*, says, " The town was prob-ably named from James Murray, the second Duke of Athol, Lord Privy Seal of Scotland."

nances Thereto belonging, he being Joyntly Oblidged Together with my Son Aaron Jones, before Named, to pay the Legacy⁵ above mentioned, and to pay my Debts & Funerall Charges, &c., and I also give to him yᵉ other Moiety of my Stock and Moveables Not before Willed.

I do also Constitute and appoint my Two Sons, Aaron and Isaac Jones, to be my Executors of This my Will, in full power and Trust, Joyntly, hereby putting into their hands all my money⁵, Bills, Bonds, and Debts, Whatsoever, and Wheresoever They are. Heartily recomending Them and all my Children to the Favour and Blessing of A gracious God.

I have Confirmed this my last Will and Testament, Renouncing and revokeing all Others, This Twentieth day of November, Anno. Domi. one Thousand Seven Hundred and Fifty Three.

Signed Sealed and Declared To be The Last Will & Testament of James Jones, in presence of

    James Mirick.

    Elisha Jones.

    Jonas Harrington, Juʳ.

James Jones

Oct. 23, 1770. The Will of James Jones, late of Weston, Gentleman, deceased, was presented for Probate by Aaron Jones & Isaac Jones the Executors. Elisha Jones & Jonas Harrington, junʳ, made oath.

                    S: DANFORTH.

Children of JAMES and SARAH (Moore) JONES.

  ✕16. JAMES,⁴ b. about 1705 ; d. at North Carolina about 1755.

    17. SARAH,⁴ b. Oct. 15, 1708 ; m. Feb. 1733-4, William Robinson, of Newton.

18. LYDIA,[4] b. Dec. 17, 1710 ; m. July 31, 1735, Capt. Stephen
Jones, of Falmouth, son of Nathaniel (9). He was Sur-
veyor General of Nova Scotia ; was a sea captain and a
captain in the army. He settled in Falmouth, near his
brother Phineas, with whom he was connected in business. He enlisted as a Captain in Col. Noble's regiment,
for an expedition against Quebec in 1746, but the ships
and troops from England did not arrive, which defeated
the project, and Col. Noble was ordered with his regiment
to Minas, now Horton, in Nova Scotia, to keep the neu-
tral French, who lived there, in subjection. The French
still kept a fort at Cumberland Bay. A considerable de-
tachment was sent from that fort, more than a hundred
miles, to attack Col. Noble's party by surprise, in a heavy
snow-storm, in the night of Jan. 7, 1746. The enemy got
very near the Colonel's quarters, where he and most of his
officers were, before they were discovered by the sentinel
at the door, by reason of the violence of the storm. The
sentinel gave the alarm and fled. Capt. Jones immedi-
ately met the enemy at the door, and was killed. They
entered the house and killed some of the officers before
they were out of bed. Col. Noble was among the slain.
The main body of the force, at some distance from the Colonel's quarters, soon after capitulated. Capt. Jones left a
widow, two sons, and two daughters. (Bond's *Watertown*,
page 311.) The sons were Stephen, Jr., and Micah.
Stephen, Chief Judge of the county of Washington, died

in Boston in 1824 or 5, aged nearly 90, according to the *Memorial of the Centennial Anniversary of the settlement of Machias*, page 101, which see. Micah died young. One of the daughters married Dea. Lyman, of Northampton, and the other, Mr. Barnard, of Deerfield.

19. EPHRAIM,[4] b. Dec. 11, 1712 ; admitted to the first church, Weston, Feb. 29, 1735–6 ; dismissed to Falmouth, May 8, 1743. He was a sea captain. His buildings were burned by the British troops in 1775. He died about the year 1783, aged 71.

20. ELIZABETH,[4] b. March 25, 1715 ; m. March 23, 1741–2, Capt. Samuel Baldwin, of Sudbury. She was dismissed from Weston church to that of Falmouth, May 8, 1743, and they returned to Weston the next year. She died July 7, 1757, and he m. in 1758 (published Jan. 21), Sarah Demind, of Needham. She died May 2, 1760, and he m. (published Feb. 22), 1762, Rebecca Cotton, of Newton. He died July 22, 1778, aged 61, and his widow m. Dec. 3, 1780, James Cogswell. Capt. Baldwin and his first wife, Elizabeth, had seven children, Samuel, born in Falmouth, Elizabeth, born in Weston (m. Elias Jones, of East Hoosack, Adams, Dec. 22, 1768, son of Col. Elisha Jones, of Weston ; had 8 children), Lydia, Ephraim, Sarah, Lucy, Esther. Capt. B. had 4 children by his second and third wives.

21. MARY,[4] b. March 16, 1716–17, m. Feb. 24, 1736–7, Elisha Flagg (bap. in Weston, Oct. 4, 1713), son of Thomas and Rebecca (Sanger) Flagg.

22. ABIGAIL,[4] b. March 14, 1718-19; m. Aug. 11, 1743, David
    Sanderson (b. June 4, 1715), son of Deacon Jonathan
    and Abigail (Fiske) Sanderson. David Sanderson was a
    deacon of the church in Petersham, where he died. Chil-
    dren, David, Ebenezer, and perhaps others.

23. CATHERINE,[4] b. April 23, 1721; m. May 24, 1743, Rev. Jo-
    seph Davis, of Holden. He was born in Lexington in
    1720; grad. H. C. 1740; settled in Holden Dec. 22,
    1742; resigned Oct. 18, 1772; died March 4, 1799.

X24. AARON,[4] b. June 10, 1723; died in Templeton, April 19,
    1820, in the 97th year of his age.

25. SOLOMON,[4] b. Jan. 30, 1726; died in Weston, Aug. 11, 1741.

26. ISAAC,[4] b. Sept. 29, 1728; m. Sept. 20, 1753, Anna Cutler
    (b. March 6, 1729-30), daughter of Ebenezer and Anna
    (Whitney) Cutler. He m. 2d (pub. Jan. 20), 1762, widow
    Mary Willis, of Medford. He had 10 children, Isaac,
    Elizabeth, Lucy, Hepzibah, Mary, William Pitt, Sarah,
    Martha, Anna, Eunice; three probably by the first wife
    and seven by the second. He was a Captain, and a
    member of the Legislature of Massachusetts. He died
    about the year 1814, aged 86.

—— 16 ——

JAMES,[4] (*James*,[3] *Josiah*,[2] *Lewis*,[1]) son of James and Sarah
    (Moore) Jones, was born in Weston about the year 1705;
    m. Dec. 26, 1728, Abigail Garfield (b. March 5, 1707-8),

dau. of Benoni and Abigail (Stearns) Garfield. Mr. Jones, when young, was a commissioned officer in a company of cavalry. With his second son, James, he went to North Carolina, when the latter was about 17 years of age. The father never returned. He died about the year 1750.

Children of JAMES and ABIGAIL (Garfield) JONES.

27. LEMUEL,5 b. May 20, 1729, in Weston; m. (pub. Sept. 28), 1754, Anna Stimpson (b. Nov. 27, 1733), dau. of James and Sarah (Cutter) Stimpson, and sister of Rev. Daniel Stimpson, grad. H. C., 1759, minister of Winchendon; d. Aug. 20, 1768. Lemuel and Anna had ten children, Amos, James, Leonard, Lemuel, Garfield, Sarah, Enoch, Anna, Ruth, Daniel. Lemuel Jones, the father, died in the year 1776.

28. JAMES,5 b, June 9, 1731; removed to North Carolina, married and had six children.

29. ABIGAIL,5 b. April 26, 1733; m. Col. Paul Raymond, of Winchendon; had six sons and one daughter, all married.

30. EUNICE,5 b. Sept. 15, 1735; m. Oct. 17, 1754, Lieut. Caleb Myrick, of Princeton (b. Sept. 30, 1728), son of James and Mary (Woolson) Myrick or Mirick. She died in 1793. They had two sons and five daughters.

31. SARAH,5 b. Aug. 3, 1737; m. May 20, 1762, Elisha Gale, of Princeton (b. Jan. 1, 1735–6), youngest son and child of Abraham and Esther (Cunningham) Gale, of Weston.

They had two sons and three daughters. The second husband of Sarah (Jones) Gale was Samuel Moore, of Worcester. They had one son.

X32. JONATHAN,[5] b. June 15, 1739 or 40 ; d. Aug. 2, 1803.

33. SOLOMON,[5] b. Feb. 8, 1741 or 42 ; m. March 14, 1764, Beulah Stratton (b. Jan. 17, 1744), dau. of Jonathan and Dinah (Bemis) Stratton, of Weston. They had *Moses,*[6] b. Jan. 20, 1765.

—— 24 ——

AARON,[4] (*James,*[3] *Josiah,*[2] *Lewis,*[1]) son of James and Sarah (Moore) Jones, born in Weston, June 10, 1723 ; m. (pub. Nov. 25), 1749, Silence Cutting, daughter of Robert and Abigail (Sawin) Cutting, of Weston, afterwards of Sudbury. She died Dec. 13, 1763, and he m. (2d), Nov. 6, 1767, Elizabeth Prescott, dau. of Col. Charles Prescott, of Concord. She died in childbed, April 27, 1770, and he married a third wife, Miriam Brewer, supposed April 29th, 1771 or 72, who died of a cancer, Nov. 8, 1790. In 1754, Aaron Jones was one of the five surveyors and collectors in Weston, his name coming first. March 6, 1758, Aaron Jones and Samuel Baldwin were chosen Constables in Weston. They both "hired" Samuel Train to serve for them. " He was accepted by the town, and sworn at the same time money oath, and oath of office." And here it may be well to state, that it was customary in those times for the town authorities to fine a man for refusing or neg-

lecting to attend to an office to which he had been legally
chosen by his townsmen. In this case, it appears, the
town accepted one man as a substitute for two, and they
jointly paid him for his services. Mr. Jones was one of
the principal proprietors of the town of Templeton, and
greatly assisted in its first settlement.* He inherited his

---

* Those who had done service in King Philip's War, as it was called, against
the Narraganset tribe of Indians, made claim for compensation. The General
Court of Massachusetts, in 1728, and subsequently in 1732, granted seven townships, each six miles square, for those soldiers and their heirs. This was confirmed
April 18, 1735. There were 840 persons entered as officers and soldiers. These
townships were divided into lots, a hundred and twenty proprietors in each township.
Narraganset, No. 6, included Templeton, and the greater part of the present town of
Phillipston. Surveys were made at an early day, and proprietor's lots were laid out,
containing 40 acres each, "of the best of the upland." These were called "house-
lots." The division was made in 1735. The committee appointed by the proprietors to lay out the lots consisted of Samuel Chandler, *James Jones* (father of Aaron,
above), Joshua Richardson, John Longley, and Joseph Fassett. Jonas Houghton
and Messrs. Hosmer, Jones, and Farrar were paid June 25, 1735, for their services
as surveyors. The "house-lot" drawn by James Jones was numbered 99.

In the Act of Incorporation, March 6, 1762, the town is called Templetown. It
is so spelled in the earliest town records, and in the first official business transac-
tions. After February, 1764, the name always appeared as *Templeton* in the town-
meeting warrant. The town, it is supposed, was named in honor of John Temple,
who then represented the American branch of the family of Richard Grenville (Earl
Temple). Nason's *Gazetteer.*

The above account was drawn chiefly from the Discourse delivered Dec. 9,
1855, by Rev. Edwin G. Adams, in commemoration of the one hundredth anniversary of the formation of the First Congregational Church in Templeton, Mass.

father's mansion in Weston; removed from Weston to Templeton, in 1772, but for many years before that time used to send necessary stores, such as salt, clothing, &c., to the first settlers, which they greatly needed, and an easy opportunity was given them to pay him for such articles. Mr. Jones built the first potash works in Templeton. He was in early life promoted from a private, in the military company, to a Lieutenant, and thence to that of a Captain. As a specimen of his losses by the depreciation of paper money, during the war of the Revolution, it may be mentioned, that he sold an excellent lot of new land, of one hundred and forty acres, in that part of Templeton which is now Gerry, and the price he received for it was insufficient to pay a soldier he hired to serve for him in the army for seven months. He lost much, also, by debts due from the first settlers of Templeton, and by continued sickness in his family. In the year 1791, his eye sight wholly failed him, and he was blind the rest of his days. Mr. Jones died in Templeton, April 19, 1820, aged nearly 97 years. He had 12 children by his three wives.

Children of AARON and SILENCE (Cutting) JONES.

34. LYDIA,[5] b. in Weston, March 23, 1752; m. April 4, 1771, Jonathan (32) Jones, son of James and Abigail (Garfield) Jones.
35. ABIGAIL,[5] b. in Weston, Nov. 29, 1754. She m. John Locke, March 8, 1778. She was his third wife. He died in Tem-

pleton, June 11, 1781. They had one child, Abigail, b. Oct. 31, 1779. She died March 20, 1866, aged 86 years. Mrs. Locke m. Benjamin Reed, March 9, 1791. He died Dec. 25, 1823. She died Sept. 21, 1839.

36. SOLOMON,⁵ b. in Weston, Aug. 29, 1757 ; d. April 29, 1758.

37. EUNICE,⁵ b. in Weston, March 21, 1759. She d. in Templeton, Jan. 9, 1837.

✕38. AARON,⁵ b. in Weston, Aug. 29, 1761 ; d. in Templeton, Oct. 22, 1828.

Children of AARON and ELIZABETH (Prescott) JONES.

39. ELIZABETH,⁵ b. in Weston, Oct. 27, 1768 ; d. Mar. 26, 1770.

✕40. PRESCOTT,⁵ b. in Weston, April 20, 1770 ; d. April 19, 1828.

Children of AARON and MIRIAM (Brewer) JONES.

41. JOSIAH,⁵ b. in Templeton, Feb. 17, 1774 ; d. Mar. 16, 1774.

✕42. LUCY,⁵ b. in Templeton, June 12, 1775 ; d. Aug. 27, 1854.

43. OLIVE,⁵ b. in Templeton, Jan. 12, 1777.

✕44. JAMES,⁵ b. in Templeton, March 30, 1779 ; d. March 1, 1831.

45. BETSEY BREWER,⁵ b. in Templeton, Sept. 17, 1784.

—— 32 ——

JONATHAN,⁵ (*James,*⁴ *James,*³ *Josiah,*² *Lewis,*¹) son of James and Abigail (Garfield) Jones, born in Weston, June 15, 1739 ; m. April 4, 1771, Lydia (34) Jones (b. March 23, 1752), dau. of Aaron and Silence (Cutting) Jones. He

died in Gerry, now Phillipston, Mass., Aug. 2, 1803.
She died in Warwick, Mass., Oct. 30, 1828, aged 76
years.   They had seven sons and four daughters, all born
in Gerry.   Their eldest child, Nahum, was an instructor
of youth.   At the time of his father's death he was
teaching school at Provincetown, on Cape Cod.   The following is copied from his diary, with slight abridgements,
under date of Thursday, Aug. 25, 1803.

"This evening I received a letter by which I had the
melancholy and heavy news of the death of my father,
Jonathan Jones.   He died on the 2d instant, of dropsy,
aged sixty-three.   In his death my mother and her ten
children mourn the loss of an affectionate husband and
parent.   Though he is taken from us, never to return, yet
we hope that he is gone to everlasting happiness in a better world.

"I wish that we, his children, may seriously consider
and duly lay to heart the dispensation of Divine Provi-
dence in our father's death; that we may imitate whatever
was praiseworthy in him; that we may be awakened to a
sense of the great importance of living lives of true piety
and virtue; of acting faithfully the parts assigned to us
in this world, that finally we may receive the rewards of
the faithful.

"My father was born at Weston, near Boston, June 15,
1740.   About the year 1770 he removed to that part of
Templeton which is now called Gerry, where he lived until

his death. He was a very industrious man, and attentive
to his business. He was sociable, hospitable, and kind to
the poor and distressed. He was a friend to good order
in society, and had a great regard for religion. He exerted himself as to the public and religious interest of the
town in which he lived.

"Gerry was from the years 1774 to 1786 the Second or
West Parish of Templeton. On the 26th of October,
1786, it was incorporated into a town. When my father
first came to this place, what is now Gerry, was quite in a
state of nature. The society was yet to be incorporated ;
a meeting-house to be built and a minister to be settled ;
school-houses to be erected, and roads to be made. The
settlement was in its infancy, and most of the inhabitants
were living too remote from any meeting-house to attend
public worship with convenience. The meeting-house
was erected in 1784 and the first minister settled in 1788.
A considerable number of the inhabitants were greatly
disaffected, and were much opposed to the building of the
meeting-house, to the incorporation of the town, and to
settling a minister. Add to these, the times were hard,
on account of the war between Britain and America, and
an insurrection which took place in this Commonwealth.
All these obstructions occasioned great struggles for the
building up of the town ; and required the most vigorous
exertions of those that were public spirited and zealous
in the cause. Perhaps no one individual in the town used

the exertions and spent the time and property for the public good that my father did. I am fully of the opinion that the town would never have been built up (as to incorporation, having a meeting-house, minister, &c.), so soon as it was, had it not been for my father's exertions in those respects, in which he took a very active and persevering part.

"When the first minister was settled, the town became well united, and has continued so, for the most part, ever since. It has greatly thrived and increased, and has become respectable. It has flourished greatly beyond what (twenty years ago) could possibly have been expected. My father was frequently in town business, having served as Town Clerk, Selectman, Assessor, &c., and often employed on committees. His exertions for the public good were not confined to his own town. He was zealous and active in the cause of his country. He served for a considerable time in the war between the American Colonies and Canada, which began in 1755 and ended in 1763. He exerted himself during the Revolutionary War with Great Britain. And during the insurrection in Massachusetts, in 1786 and 1787, he was particularly active and assiduous in using means for the suppression of the insurrection, and the restoration of good order."

Lydia, wife of Jonathan Jones, removed to Warwick, Mass., in the autumn of the year 1815, and had her home with her son George, until her death, Oct. 30, 1828. She

was a superior woman, possessing many excellent traits of character. She had a pleasant disposition, was quiet and retiring in her deportment. In every relation of life she was an example eminently beautiful and good. A member of the church from early life, she was in the highest sense a christian. She greatly assisted her husband in his duties and labors for society, and in educating a large family of children.

Children of JONATHAN and LYDIA (Jones) JONES.

×46. NAHUM,[6] b. Aug. 13, 1772 ; d. Oct. 22, 1807, aged 35 years.

47. LYDIA,[6] b. Sept. 16, 1774 ; d. Nov. 17, 1853, aged 79 years.

×48. AMOS,[6] b. Feb. 14, 1777 ; d. at the West, in 1816 or 1817.

49. JONATHAN,[6] b. July 3, 1779 ; d. Sept. 5, 1869, aged 90 years. He married Polly Currier, of Conway, Mass., Oct. 18, 1811. They had no child. She died May 24, 1870, aged 88 years.

50. NABBY,[6] b. Aug. 15, 1781 ; d. June 7, 1782.

×51. CYRUS,[6] b. April 22, 1783 ; d. in 1826 or 1827.

52. NABBY,[6] b. July 23, 1785 ; d. Dec. 25, 1832.

53. MARY,[6] b. April 29, 1788 ; d. Aug. 7, 1876, aged 88 years. She married John Boyden, of Conway (his second marriage), May, 1835. He died Oct. 22, 1857, aged 93 years.

×54. GEORGE,[6] b. Aug. 1, 1790 ; d. March 13, 1869, aged 78 years.

55. JEFFREY AMHERST,[6] b. Jan. 24, 1793 ; d. Feb. 8, 1840, aged 47 years.

×56. JAMES,[6] b. Oct. 30, 1795 ; d. Dec. 3, 1826, aged 31 years.

—— 38 ——

AARON,[5] (*Aaron*,[4] *James*,[3] *Josiah*,[2] *Lewis*,[1]) son of Aaron and
Silence (Cutting) Jones, was born in Weston, Aug. 29,
1761. He married Betsey Bush in 1785. She was born
Feb. 18, 1761, and died Sept. 24, 1834. He died in
Templeton, Oct. 22, 1828, aged 66 years. They had
eight children, all born in Templeton, Mass.

Children of AARON and BETSEY (Bush) JONES.

57. STEPHEN,[6] b. July 7, 1786; died unmarried.
58. POLLY,[6] b. March 15, 1789; died unmarried.
59. AARON,[6] b. July 30, 1791; died unmarried.
60. BETSEY,[6] b. Dec. 29, 1794; m. Herman Partridge.
61. AUGUSTUS APPLETON,[6] b. Jan. 24, 1797; m. Mary Partridge.
X62. GEORGE WASHINGTON,[6] b. May 11, 1799.
63. ABIGAIL,[6] b. Dec. 23, 1801; m. Samuel Abbott.

—— 40 ——

PRESCOTT,[5] (*Aaron*,[4] *James*,[3] *Josiah*,[2] *Lewis*,[1]) son of Aaron
and Elizabeth (Prescott) Jones, was born in Weston, April
20, 1770; m. Jan. 31, 1798, Jane Moore (b. at Cambridge, Jan. 14, 1769). He died April 19, 1828, aged
57 years. She died May 26, 1835, aged 66 years.

Children of PRESCOTT and JANE (Moore) JONES.

X64. JOSIAH MOORE,[6] b. Jan. 13, 1800.
65. PRESCOTT,[6] b. Jan. 27, 1802; d. Dec. 3, 1839, aged 37 years.

X66. FREDERICK,[6] b. Aug. 31, 1803.

67. WILLIAM,[6] b. Oct. 21, 1805 ; d. Nov. 4, 1813, aged 8 years.

X68. OTIS,[6] b. June 26, 1807.

X69. JANE,[6] b. June 16, 1809.

70. EDWIN,[6] b. July 15, 1811 ; d. Oct. 1, 1813.

—— 42 ——

LUCY,[5] (*Aaron,*[4] *James,*[3] *Josiah,*[2] *Lewis,*[1]) daughter of Aaron and Miriam (Brewer) Jones, was born in Templeton, Mass., June 12, 1775 ; married Lipha French, Jan. 24, 1798. He died Nov. 10, 1845. She died Aug. 27, 1854. They had seven children, all born in Templeton.

Children of LIPHA and LUCY (Jones) FRENCH.

71. LUCY FRENCH,[6] b. Dec. 24, 1798; m. John W. Work, of Templeton, Jan. 23, 1840 ; d. Dec. 8, 1857. They had no children.

72. HARRIET FRENCH,[6] b. Dec. 6, 1800 ; d. Aug. 17, 1813.

73. CHARLES FRENCH,[6] b. Dec. 19, 1802 ; d. Aug. 10, 1824.

74. LOUISA BREWER FRENCH,[6] b. March 6, 1805 ; d. Aug. 7, 1833.

75. INFANT CHILD,[6] b. June 6, 1807 ; d. June 6, 1807.

76. PRESCOTT FRENCH,[6] b. Sept. 12, 1808 ; d. Dec. 28, 1846.

77. OLIVE FRENCH,[6] b. Dec. 10, 1810; d. Oct. 4, 1811.

—— 44 ——

JAMES,[5] (*Aaron,*[4] *James,*[3] *Josiah,*[2] *Lewis,*[1]) son of Aaron and Miriam (Brewer) Jones, born in Templeton, Mass., March

30, 1779 ; m. Feb. 16, 1819, Christiana Hubbard Field, dau. of Zachariah and Abigail Mattoon Field, born in Northfield, Mass., Oct. 11, 1796. James Jones died at Windsor, Vt., March 1, 1831.

Children of JAMES and CHRISTIANA HUBBARD (Field) JONES.

X 78. HARRIET MARIA,[6] b. in Windsor, Vt., Nov. 29, 1819.

79. CATHERINE FIELD,[6] b. in Windsor, Oct. 19, 1822.

X 80. JAMES BREWER,[6] b. in Windsor, March 31, 1826.

—— 46 ——

NAHUM,[6] (*Jonathan,*[5] *James,*[4] *James,*[3] *Josiah,*[2] *Lewis,*[1]) son of Jonathan and Lydia (Jones) Jones, was born Aug. 13, 1772. His education, at first, was such as the common schools afforded, being only a few weeks in the year. He was a good scholar and learned rapidly, especially in arithmetic. He attended school, and labored on his father's farm, until he was eighteen years of age, and on the 27th of December, 1790, commenced his first school in Winchendon, Mass ; he had eighty-eight scholars. The young man continued to teach in different parts of the town of Winchendon in 1790 to 1793, and gave good satisfaction. In 1794 and 1795 he was teacher in Rindge, N. H. In the autumn of 1792 he attended the academy at New Ipswich, N. H.

In the latter part of the year 1792 he was for some

time in the academy at Leicester, Mass. In the year 1794 he joined the academy connected with Williams College, in Williamstown. In April, 1795, Mr. Jones decided to make a journey to the State of New York, with a view of school teaching, the object being to teach a school there in summer and winter. He made the journey on foot, carrying his baggage. From Gerry to Albany was 111 miles; from Albany to Paris, N. Y., 100; the whole distance, 211 miles. He kept a "diary" from early life to nearly its close. The preceding, and much that follows, is selected from it.

May 18, 1795, he began his first school in New York State, in the town of Florida, Montgomery County, twenty miles from Schenectady. The inhabitants are low Dutch.

1795. Aug. 13. This day I am twenty-three years of age. How swiftly life passes away! To look back on twelve or fourteen years of my life, how short the time appears! Like a dream. The days of one's life, at most, are very soon over! With what diligence and care should the fleeting moments be employed. How many that were of my age and acquaintance are now no more! (in this world). I am mercifully spared, but am sensible of the uncertainty of seeing another birth-day. Serious matters, these. Every one, as they grow older, ought, by all means, to endeavor to become better.

Sept., 1795. Went to Whitestown, N. Y. It is settled by New England people; is 220 miles west from Gerry.

Oct. 1, 1795.   Returned to Gerry, on foot, very much
fatigued.   Arrived at his father's house in six days.

1797. Jan. 1.   How rapidly the years, and even the
centuries, roll away.   A new year has now commenced.
The present century will soon be completed.   Of what
great consequence it is to employ all our time to the best
advantage.

Feb. 10, 1797.   Whitestown, County of Herkimer, N. Y.
Received letters from Gerry.   Have not heard from there
since last June.

1797. March 9.   Exhibition of school, which gave
great satisfaction to the Commissioners and people.   Said
to be the best school, and the foremost in learning of any
in this part of the State.   School closed, and commenced
another in Paris, N. Y., 7 miles from Whitestown.   En-
gage for one year ; wages, one hundred and eighty-two
dollars, and board.

Apr. 30.   Two years, this day, since I set out from
Gerry for this country.   How rapid the flight of time.

Sept. 30.   Returned to Gerry ; arrived home Oct. 5th,
in the evening, having walked all the way, except sixteen
miles.

Oct. 23.   Went to Rutland, Mass., on foot, and back
the same day ; distance, 40 miles.

Nov. 6.   Returned to Paris, N. Y., on foot, in a little
more than six days.   Stood the fatigues of the journey,
both ways, very well.

1798. May 10. Closed school in Paris, N. Y. Kept the school one year. Exhibition was very satisfactory ; above fifty pieces, orations and dialogues were spoken. One hundred and seventy scholars in this school, in all ; the greater part were young.

May 14, 1798. Began a school in Whitestown, N. Y., (where he kept one year and a half, from Aug. 25, 1795, to March 23, 1797). He taught this time, forty-two weeks.

June 11, 1799. Began a school in Florida, N. Y., and continued three months, it being the same he taught in 1795. The scholars were low Dutch.

1799. August 13. This day arrive to the age of twenty-seven years.

November 11. He returned home from New York for the last time. Mr. Jones now purchased the home farm of the Rev. Ebenezer Tucker, in Gerry. Said farm contained ninety acres, situated half a mile south of the meeting-house, and adjoining his father's farm.

November 18, 1799. Began to teach in the Federal school-house (so called), in the south part of the town, where he used to go as a scholar in 1790, and a year or two preceding that time. Among his scholars were six brothers and two sisters, all younger than himself.

1800. March 11. Took possession of his farm and commenced housekeeping, his sister Lydia being his housekeeper. Mr. Jones continued laboring on his farm until November 4, 1801, when he began a school in Winchendon, where he taught eight weeks.

March 2, 1801. Chosen Selectman and Town Clerk of the town of Gerry.

March 18, 19 and 30th. Look over and arrange papers belonging to the town, which I find very much deranged. In September he was much interested in instituting a social library for the town.

1801. November. Continued teaching and laboring on his farm. Took an active part in establishing a social library in Gerry, and was chosen one of the trustees, committee for purchasing books, &c.

1802. April. Leased his farm and engaged in school-teaching. The remainder of this year and of the years 1803 and 1804 were occupied in teaching school at Provincetown, Cape Cod. He made frequent journeys to Gerry and back, always on foot, walking thirty to forty miles a day.

1805. March 2. He left the Cape for the last time; returned to Gerry and labored on his own farm and for his brother Amos. Mr. Jones began teaching school December 27, 1790, when eighteen years old, and the last school he taught closed March 17, 1807. He instructed in all, ten years and six weeks. The total number of scholars were fourteen hundred and fifty-six. Their names are all contained in a register he kept, each school by itself. He was very successful as a teacher, and gave good satisfaction. He was a remarkably industrious man. His "diary" shows every day occupied. His fatiguing travels on foot probably injured his health. He was a member of the church and a constant attendant on public worship, wherever residing. He took great interest in town, state and national affairs, as appears in his "diary," and ever gave his influence in favor of morality and religion. Mr. Jones never married. He died Oct. 22, 1807, aged 35 years.

—— 48 ——

AMOS,[6] (*Jonathan,*[5] *James,*[4] *James,*[3] *Josiah,*[2] *Lewis,*[1]) son of Jonathan and Lydia (Jones) Jones, was born Feb. 14, 1777 ; m. June 9, 1806, Louisa Maynard, dau. of Gardner and Anna (Ross) Maynard, (b. in Gerry, April 30, 1783). She died Oct. 15, 1809. aged 26 years. The second marriage of Amos Jones was to Mary Rice, Aug. 29, 1810. She was a daughter of Asa and Miriam (Wheeler) Rice, born in Shrewsbury, Feb. 23, 1784. She died Sept. 4, 1864, aged 80 years. He died at the West in 1816 or 1817, aged about 40 years.

Children of Amos and Louisa (Maynard) Jones.

81. Nahum,[7] b. in Gerry, Dec. 22, 1807.
82. Permelia Louisa,[7] b. in Gerry, March 13, 1809 ; d. Feb. 12, 1859, aged 50 years.

Children of Amos and Mary (Rice) Jones.

83. Amos Bascom,[7] b. in Gerry, July 15, 1811.
84. George Henry,[7] b. in Gerry, April 2, 1813.

—— 51 ——

CYRUS,[6] (*Jonathan,*[5] *James,*[4] *James,*[3] *Josiah,*[2] *Lewis,*[1]) son of
Jonathan and Lydia (Jones) Jones, was born April 22,
1783 ; married Sally Bowker, of Gerry, May 22, 1810.
She was born Nov. 14, 1789 ; died at Hinsdale, N. H.,
Aug. 15, 1841, aged 51 years. He died in 1826 or 1827.

Child of Cyrus and Sally (Bowker) Jones.

85. Henry Mason,[7] b. in Gerry, July 24, 1811.

—— 54 ——

GEORGE,[6] (*Jonathan,*[5] *James,*[4] *James,*[3] *Josiah,*[2] *Lewis,*[1]) son
of Jonathan and Lydia (Jones) Jones, was born August 1,
1790 ; m. Eliza Richards, Jan. 16, 1820. She died in
Warwick, Mass., April 26, 1863, aged 69 years. They
had five children, born in Warwick. He died in Winches-
ter, N.H., March 13, 1869, aged 78 years.

Children of George and Eliza (Richards) Jones.

86. Elizabeth,[7] b. April 22, 1821.
87. Martha Caroline,[7] b. March 4, 1824 ; d. Dec. 5, 1862,
     aged 38 years.
88. James Amherst,[7] b. August 7, 1826.

89. HANNAH ZIBIAH,[7] b. May 3, 1829; d. Sept. 4, 1864, aged 25 years.

90. LOUISA PERMELIA,[7] b. Nov. 12, 1832.

—— 56 ——

JAMES,[6] (*Jonathan*,[5] *James*,[4] *James*,[3] *Josiah*,[2] *Lewis*,[1]) son of Jonathan and Lydia (Jones) Jones, born Oct. 30, 1795; m. September 17, 1822, Susannah Goddard, of Brookline, Mass., daughter of Joseph and Mary (Aspinwall) Goddard, born Sept. 17, 1794. Their children were born in Roxbury. He died Dec. 3, 1826, aged 31 years.

Children of JAMES and SUSANNAH (Goddard) JONES.

91. SUSANNAH GODDARD,[7] b. Jan. 30, 1823; d. Nov. 22, 1824.

92. LOUISA ELIZABETH,[7] b. Aug. 17, 1824.

93. SUSAN MARIA,[7] b. Dec. 12, 1825.

—— 61 ——

AUGUSTUS APPLETON,[6] (*Aaron*,[5] *Aaron*,[4] *James*,[3] *Josiah*,[2] *Lewis*,[1]) son of Aaron and Betsey (Bush) Jones, born Jan. 24, 1797; m. Jan. 27, 1831, Mary Partridge, b. Sept. 18, 1804; d. June 5, 1875.

Children of AUGUSTUS APPLETON and MARY (Partridge) JONES.

94. LEONARD AUGUSTUS,[7] b. Jan. 13, 1832; grad. at Harv. Coll. 1855; m. Dec. 14, 1867, Josephine Harding Lee, dau. of

Artemas Lee, of Templeton, b. Feb. 7, 1840.   Their son,
Arthur Lee,[8] was born March 9, 1869 ; d. Oct. 18, 1869.

95. JAMES LLOYD,[7] b. Aug. 12, 1834 ; d. July 15, 1838.

96. EDWARD LLOYD,[7] b. July 11, 1839 ; Capt. in 54th Massachusetts Volunteers, May 14, 1863, to Dec. 16, 1864, and se-
verely wounded in attack on Fort Sumpter ; m. Feb. 10,
1867, Susan M. Clare, of Charleston, S. C.

×97. JULIUS APPLETON,[7] b. July 6, 1843.

98. CHARLES EMMONS,[7] b. Nov. 15, 1848 ; m. Nov. 4, 1871, Ida
Wright.

—— 62 ——

GEORGE WASHINGTON,[6] (*Aaron,*[5] *Aaron,*[4] *James,*[3] *Josiah,*[2] *Lewis,*[1]) son of Aaron and Betsey (Bush) Jones,
was born May 11, 1799 ; m. Jan. 24, 1839, Caroline
Partridge.

Children of GEORGE WASHINGTON and CAROLINE (Partridge) JONES.

99. HARRIET LOUISA,[7] b. Sept. 13, 1840 ; m. Oct. 22, 1868, Dr.
John Green.

100. GEORGE IRVING,[7] b. July 17, 1847 ; grad. Harv. Coll. 1871.

101. CAROLINE ROSELLA,[7] b. April 5, 1850 ; m. March 25, 1874,
James Hanna.

—— 64 ——

JOSIAH MOORE,[6] (*Prescott,*[5] *Aaron,*[4] *James,*[3] *Josiah,*[2]
Lewis,[1]) son of Prescott and Jane (Moore) Jones, was

born Jan. 13, 1800. He m. July 1, 1829, Maria Buckminster Bullard, b. August 23, 1807. She died March
8, 1861.

Children of JOSIAH MOORE and MARIA BUCKMINSTER (Bullard) JONES.

102. AMELIA FRANCES,[7] b. April 18, 1830 ; m. Feb. 21, 1855,
George Washington Easton Wood. They have no children. He died Nov. 17, 1877.

103. GEORGE RIPLEY,[7] b. Dec. 21, 1831 ; d. Dec. 1, 1832.

104. ELLEN MARIA,[7] b. Sept. 20, 1833.

X 105. MARY BUCKMINSTER,[7] b. Sept. 6, 1835.

106. CLARENCE WILLIAM,[7] b. Dec. 22, 1837 ; m. Sarah Gavett,
Feb. 2, 1869 ; no children.

X 107. ELIZABETH PRESCOTT,[7] b. May 14, 1841.

108. ADELAIDE LOUISA,[7] b. Jan. 9, 1844.

109. FRANCIS BUCKMINSTER,[7] b. March 1, 1850.

—— 66 ——

FREDERICK,[6] (*Prescott,*[5] *Aaron,*[4] *James,*[3] *Josiah,*[2] *Lewis,*[1])
son of Prescott and Jane (Moore) Jones, was born August
31, 1803. He m. Dec. 1, 1831, in Athol, Mass., Maria
Sweetser, dau. of Samuel Sweetser, of Athol.

Children of FREDERICK and MARIA (Sweetser) JONES.

X 110. CAROLINE SWEETSER,[7] b. Oct. 28, 1835.

111. JANE MARIA,[7] b. May 28, 1837 ; d. March 16, 1858.

112. FREDERICK WILLIAM,[7] b. May 19, 1839 ; d. Sept. 9, 1839.
113. FREDERICK HENRY,[7] b. July 27, 1842 ; d. Aug. 18, 1842.

—— 68 ——

OTIS,[6] (*Prescott,*[5] *Aaron,*[4] *James,*[3] *Josiah,*[2] *Lewis,*[1]) son of
Prescott and Jane (Moore) Jones, born June 26, 1807 ; m.
Oct. 31, 1831, Harriet Stockwell.

Children of OTIS and HARRIET (Stockwell) JONES.

114. EDWIN AUGUSTUS,[7] b. Sept. 26, 1832 ; m. May 24, 1857,
Harriet Frances Todd.
115. FRANCES JANE,[7] b. June 29, 1835 ; m. May 29, 1855, Augustus Messer. They had one child, *Frederick Harold,*[8] born
Sept. 10, 1868 ; d. Jan. 30, 1878, aged 9 years.
116. PRESCOTT,[7] b. Jan. 17, 1840 ; d. Jan. 11, 1863.

—— 69 ——

JANE,[6] (*Prescott,*[5] *Aaron,*[4] *James,*[3] *Josiah,*[2] *Lewis,*[1]) daughter
of Prescott and Jane (Moore) Jones, born June 16, 1809 ;
m. Oct. 9, 1830, Charles Humphrey. He died April 25,
1860, aged 52 years.

Children of CHARLES and JANE (Jones) HUMPHREY.

117. HORATIO DWIGHT [7] HUMPHREY, b. Oct. 7, 1831.
X 118. MARY TILESTON [7] HUMPHREY, b. Sept. 28, 1834.
119. EDWARD PAYSON [7] HUMPHREY, b. Nov. 30, 1838 ; m. August

12, 1862, Mary A. Phinney. They had *Edward P.,*[8] b. Aug. 10, 1865. Mr. Humphrey died April 7, 1865, aged 26 years.

120. JANE MARIA[7] HUMPHREY, b. July 30, 1844.

121. CLARA[7] HUMPHREY, b. Sept. 24, 1846 ; m. Feb. 14, 1871, J. D. Butler. She died Sept. 23, 1872, aged 26 years.

—— 78 ——

HARRIET MARIA,[6] (*James,*[5] *Aaron,*[4] *James,*[3] *Josiah,*[2] *Lewis,*[1]) daughter of James and Christiana Hubbard (Field) Jones, born in Windsor, Vt., Nov. 29, 1819 ; m. Jan. 3, 1843, George Roswell Chapman, born at Rutland, Vt., July 6, 1816.

Children of GEORGE ROSWELL and HARRIET MARIA (Jones) CHAPMAN.

122. GEORGE KELLOGG[7] CHAPMAN, b. in Woodstock, Vt., November 4, 1843.

123. JAMES HENRY[7] CHAPMAN, b. in Woodstock, Feb. 10, 1846.

124. FREDERICK[7] CHAPMAN, b. in Woodstock, Aug. 13, 1848.

125. NANCY BATES[7] CHAPMAN, b. in Woodstock, July 25, 1850.

126. CHARLES FIELD[7] CHAPMAN, b. in Woodstock, Jan. 14, 1856.

—— 80 ——

JAMES BREWER,[6] (*James,*[5] *Aaron,*[4] *James,*[3] *Josiah,*[2] *Lewis,*[1]) son of James and Christian Hubbard (Field) Jones, born in Windsor, Vt., March 31, 1826 ; m. Oct. 10, 1859, Lucy Fitch Whitney, born at Brattleboro, Vt., Feb. 28, 1830.

Children of JAMES BREWER and LUCY FITCH (Whitney) JONES.

127. FRED. WHITNEY,[7] b. in Woodstock, Vt., Feb. 15, 1861.
128. WILLIAM FIELD,[7] b. in Woodstock, April 23, 1862.
129. MARY WELLS,[7] b. in Woodstock, July 28, 1864.
130. ELLEN HYDE,[7] b. in Woodstock, Sept. 10, 1866.

—— 97 ——

JULIUS APPLETON,[7] (*Augustus Appleton,*[6] *Aaron,*[5] *Aaron,*[4] *James,*[3] *Josiah,*[2] *Lewis,*[1]) son of Augustus Appleton and Mary (Partridge) Jones, was born July 6, 1843 ; m. Dec. 3, 1867, Aurora Lucy Randall, of Augusta, Me.

Children of JULIUS APPLETON and AURORA LUCY (Randall) JONES.

131. HERBERT RANDALL,[8] b. Jan. 26, 1869.
132. HELEN AURORA,[8] b. July 2, 1874.

—— 105 ——

MARY BUCKMINSTER JONES,[7] (*Josiah Moore,*[6] *Prescott,*[5] *Aaron,*[4] *James,*[3] *Josiah,*[2] *Lewis,*[1]) daughter of Josiah Moore and Maria Buckminster (Bullard) Jones, born Sept. 6, 1835 ; m. Oct. 20, 1858, Joseph Benjamin Moors.

Children of JOSEPH BENJAMIN and MARY BUCKMINSTER (Jones) MOORS.

133. ARTHUR WENDELL[8] MOORS, b. Nov. 14, 1859.
134. JOHN FARWELL[8] MOORS, b. Oct. 31, 1861.
135. FRANCIS JOSEPH[8] MOORS, b. Jan. 23, 1864.
136. MARIA BUCKMINSTER[8] MOORS, b. April 21, 1866.
137. ETHEL PRESCOTT[8] MOORS, b. March 28, 1869.
138. ADELAIDE JONES[8] MOORS, b. Aug. 17, 1873.

—— 107 ——

ELIZABETH PRESCOTT JONES,[7] (*Josiah Moore,[6] Prescott,[5] Aaron,[4] James,[3] Josiah,[2] Lewis,[1]*) daughter of Josiah Moore and Maria Buckminster (Bullard) Jones, born May, 14, 1841 ; m. Oct. 20, 1868, Alexander Pomeroy Sears.

Children of ALEXANDER POMEROY and ELIZABETH PRESCOTT (Jones) SEARS.

139. ELLEN WARLAND[8] SEARS, b. April 24, 1870.
140. MARGARET ALGER[8] SEARS, b. April 18, 1874.

—— 110 ——

CAROLINE SWEETSER JONES,[7] (*Frederick,[6] Prescott,[5] Aaron,[4] James,[3] Josiah,[2] Lewis,[1]*) daughter of Frederick and Maria (Sweetser) Jones, born Oct. 28, 1835 ; m. in Boston, Sept. 18, 1855, Francis Faulkner Emery.

Children of FRANCIS FAULKNER and CAROLINE SWEET-
SER (Jones) EMERY.

141. MARIA SWEETSER[8] EMERY, b. Aug. 22, 1856.
142. FRANCIS FAULKNER[8] EMERY, b. May 25, 1860.
143. EDWARD STANLEY[8] EMERY, b. Dec. 28, 1864.
144. FREDERICK JONES[8] EMERY, b. July 5, 1870 ; d. May 17, 1872.

— 118 —

MARY TILESTON[7] HUMPHREY, (*Jane,[6] Prescott,[5] Aaron,[4]
James,[3] Josiah,[2] Lewis,[1]) daughter of Charles and Jane
(Jones) Humphrey, born Sept. 28, 1834 ; m. June 26,
1862, Nelson Shumway.

Children of NELSON and MARY TILESTON (Humphrey)
SHUMWAY.

145. HAROLD HUMPHREY[8] SHUMWAY, b. March 23, 1864.
146. ALICE DWIGHT[8] SHUMWAY, b. Sept. 12, 1865.
147. ETHEL NELSON[8] SHUMWAY, b. March 19, 1868.

APPENDIX.

DOWER OF ABIGAIL (GARFIELD) JONES, 1782.

It is stated on page 27, that James[4] Jones, son of James,[3] and great-grandson of Lewis,[1] went with his second son, James,[5] to North Carolina, about the year 1748 ; that the father never returned, but died soon after. A committee was appointed to appraise the real estate of Mr. Jones, in Weston, and set off the widow's portion, as follows :

NOVEMBER 5, 1782.

Samuel Fisk, Isaac Hobbs, & Elisha Harrington, all of Weston, were appointed a Committee to apprize the real estate of James Jones, gentleman, and to set off to Abigail, the deceased's widow, one Third part of said Estate for her Dower or Thirds during her Life. The following is the return made :

MIDDLESEX, ss. *To the Honorable Oliver Prescott, Esq., Judge of Probate for said County.* Pursuant to a Commission from your Honour, Directing us, the Subscribers, to Apprize all the Real Estate whereof James Jones, Gent[n], late of Weston, in said County, Died Seized and Possessed of, and to sett of to Abigail, the Widow of said Deceased, one third part of said Estate as her right of Dower, having met on said business (all parties concerned having Notice), we Proceeded & Surveyed the premises as shown to us, which were bounded as followeth, viz.: beginning at a stake and stones at the Northeast Corner of the premises, on the line of the meadow of the heirs of Abraham Biglow, thence runing westerly to a Rock and white oak stump on the heirs above said, and on Lands of Abraham Harrington, thence south-westerly on Lands of said Harrington, to a Brook call^d four mile Brook, thence more Southerly by a Town way to the County Road, crossing the said Road, to a white Oak stump, the Corner of Samuel Fisk's Lands, thence southerly on Lands of said Fisk, one Hundred and thirty-two rods, to Lands of Joel Smith, thence Easterly on Lands of said Smith, sixty-two rods, to a walnut plant & stones, thence running Northerly on Lands of the heirs of Lemuel Jones, on a straight line, to the bounds first mentioned ; being by estimation, Ninety-seven Acres, with a Dwelling House, Barn & Cyder House Standing thereon, valued at Six Hundred Pounds, £600.oo. Having thus compleated the Inventory and Apprizement of said Estate, we Proceeded and Sett off to Abigail, the widow of said Deceased, the North westerly part of the Premises, begining at a stake and stones Directly before the front Door of said Dwelling House, thence runing Northerly in a Direct line to the middle of the Chimney of said House, thence to the Easterly end of a stone fence between said House and Barn, thence to said Barn, and through said Barn, by the westerly side of the floor-way, thence Still Northerly to a Stake and Stones by the Pasture wall, thence Westerly by said wall to a stone fence, thence Northerly by s^d fence to a fence by the side of a Meadow, thence westerly by s^d fence to a white Oak Tree (standing in a Stone fence), Marked, thence Northerly to a Rock and white oak Stump at the Corner of Abr^m Harrington's field, Bounded hitherto by the Two thirds, thence South-westerly & Southerly by Lands of s^d Harrington and a Town way, to the County Road, thence by s^d County Road to the bounds first mentioned, with all the Buildings Standing thereon, with every Privilidge to the same belonging, Reserving to the said widow & her heirs & assigns, Liberty of Passing & repassing to and from the well and Drawing water therefrom, as there may be Occation, also reserving unto said widow and the heirs of the two thirds, equal liberty of Passing Down Cellar & up Chamber, &c., into their respective part of said Dwelling House, in the best and usual way, also that the front Door be used in Common by all Parties, and each Party to have Liberty to Pass and repass on Lands of each other, from the Road to the House & Barn, as they shall have Occation, and the Barn floor to be used in Common by both parties ; also reserving unto the Heirs of the two thirds, Liberty of Passing and repassing across the Northerly part of the Premises to Cart their Hay, &c., as they may have Occation, which thirds or right of Dower is estimated at Twenty five acres, and Valued at Two Hundred and four Pounds, Ten Shillings. £204, 10, 0.

SAML. FISK,
ISAAC HOBBS,   } COMMITTEE.
ELISHA HARRINGTON,

WESTON, Dec. 27, 1782.

Middlesex, 12 March, 1783. I accept of this return & order it to be recorded.

OLIVER PRESCOTT, *J. prob.*

Countersigners,—Abigail $\times$ Jones, Amos Jones, James Jones, Lemuel Jones ; Samuel Lampson, Guardian for Sarah, Enoch, and Anna ; Matthew Hobbs, Guardian for Ruth and Daniel.

[The foregoing appears to have been in 1783, the eight living children of Lemuel Jones, deceased, the eldest son and child of James and Abigail (Garfield) Jones.]

ABSTRACTS OF WILLS, INVENTORIES, ETC., FROM THE PROBATE OFFICE, EAST CAMBRIDGE.

Extract from the will of Samuel Jones, of Weston, Firmed in Weston, Jan. 14, 1717-18, Mentions sons Saml. & Moses, who were minors.

In Testimony of my regard to the Publ. worship of God, And from yᵉ sense I have of the need there is of a larger Meeting House in this Town, I freely give and bequeath to this Town of Weston, towards such a good work, the sum of Twenty pounds in Province Bills of Credit, or money as it shall then pass, to be paid by my Heirs or Executrs, when that service demands it, In case my Estate may be freed from any Public Tax thereunto, and it be set in or near the place or Lott where the present Meetg House stands.

In Token of the honr & respect which I bear to Mr. Williams, the Pastor of the Church in this Town, I freely give & bequeath towards the educatn of his son, the sum of Five pounds, or for any other pious use that he shall see cause, to be paid by my Heirs or Executr.

Will proved, April 9, 1718.

Elizabeth Jones, jun., widow, Solomon Park & Ebenezer Littlefield, Husbandmen, all of Holliston, in the County of Middlesex, are bound unto Jonathan Remington, Esq., Judge of the Probate of Wills, in the sum of one thousand Pounds.   Aug. 30, 1742.

Dec. 2, 1789. Thaddeus Spring appointed Administrator of the estate of Abigail Jones, late of Weston, widow, dec^d, intestate.

Gerry, May 4, 1789. I, Jonathan Jones, of Gerry, having been appointed Guardian for Ruth Jones, Minor Daughter to Lemuel Jones, of Weston, dec^d, it appears that there is some estate yet unsettled, being ye thirds of widow Abigail Jones, now deceased, who was grandmother to Ruth Jones, if it be necessary that there be an Administrator appointed to settle the above mentioned estate, I am perfectly willing to consent to ye appointment of any person whom your honors & the other Heirs shall elect & appoint as administrators to settle s^d Estate, as witness my hand.

JONATHAN JONES,
Guardian to s^d Ruth Jones.

ABSTRACTS OF DEEDS—JOSIAH JONES, GRANTEE AND GRANTOR.

Deed from Nathaniel Tredway, to John Livermore, Richard Child, Josiah Jones, of Watertowne, and John Hayward, of Concord, 30 acres in Wattertowne, and is part of that tract of land commonly called or going under the denomination of law of township.

April 21, 1684. Josiah Jones to John Bright. All my part and share of the Mills at Stony Brook, which is one-quarter part of the whole purchase, namely, Thirty acres of land bought of Nathaniel Tredway, as appears by a Deed made to me, Josiah Jones, and the rest of my partners, bearing date the Nineteenth day of February, one thousand six hundred seaventy-eight, and another parcell of land bought of John Chadwick. (See pages 12 and 13.) Middlesex Deeds, ix. 336.

ABSTRACT OF WILL OF JOSIAH JONES, OF BOSTON, 1744-5.

Jan. 15, 1744-5. Josiah Jones, of Boston, mariner, to dau -in-law, Lucretia Simpson, £50, old tenor ; to other dau.-in-law, Ann Adams, £50, old tenor, when effects come from N. Carolina, or before, if my wife is enabled so to do. All the rest of my estate in Carolina and Boston, to my wife, Mary Jones, now remaining in Boston. At my wife's death, I would have all that remains given to and go to the Poor of Doct^r. Cutler's Church, for their help through this world, and to be paid to proper Persons at my Wife's Death, for that end. Wife Mary, Mr. Samuel Grant, and Mr. Joseph Sherburne, Executors. Will proved Feb. 12, 1744-5. Suffolk Probate Records, vol. 37, p. 420.

THE TWO LOTS OF JAMES JONES, IN NARRAGANSETT TOWNSHIP.

It will be seen (page 22), that James Jones, in his will, made in 1753, gives lot No. 5, in Narragansett township, No 6, to his son Aaron, and lot No. 99, drawn by him, to his youngest son Isaac. The " forty-acre lot, " No. 5, was drawn by John Overing, Esq., in 1735, according to the list given in the appendix to the historical discourse by Rev. Mr. Adams, page 89. It may have been that James Jones obtained this lot by purchase from Mr. Overing, or some other party authorized to dispose of it.

EXTRACTS FROM RECORD BOOK OF TOWN OF WESTON, MASS.

The Book of Records of the First Precinct in Weston, Dec. 11th, A. D., 1746. " Whereas, by an Order of the Great and General

Court of the Province of the Massachusetts Bay, passed the 26th of April Last, a Number of the Inhabitants of Weston, With Others, Inhabitants of Concord and Lexington, are set off to be a Separate precinct, and Thereby the remaining part of the said Town of Weston is an entire parrish.

These are therefore to Request your Hon^r would Issue a Warrant for Calling the first precinct Meeting in the first precinct of Weston, to Choose precinct Officers, as The Law Directs.

James Mirick,	Nathaniel Allen,
Jon^a. Bullard,	Abijah Upham,
John Walker,	John Hasting,
Daniel Livermore,	Elisha Jones."

Meeting called Dec. 11, 1746. Elisha Jones chosen Precinct Clerk.

Mr. John Jones, for Twenty-six feet of slit work, for ye meeting-house stairs, at 9d per foot, 19s, 6d.

1755. Abraham Jones, tything man. Dea. Upham, Capt. Elisha Jones, and Mr. John Jones, a committee about the school house. Mr. John Jones on a Committee to sell or divide the Farm belonging to the Towns of Watertown, Weston and Waltham.

1756. Meeting to hear the report of the Committee, appointed to Joyn with a Committee of Watertown and Waltham, to make sale of said Town Farm, near Watchuset Hill. Sold share for £267, 6, 8. Elisha Jones, Treasurer and Town Clerk.

1757. Aaron Jones, tything man.

1758. Elisha Jones, Representative to General Court, and in 1760 and 1762.

1760. Nathan Jones, Isaac Jones, tithing men.

EXTRACT FROM BARDSLEY'S ENGLISH SURNAMES.

The surnames from John are as multifarious as is possible in the case of a monosyllable, ingenuity in the contraction thereof being thus manifestly limited. As "John," simple, it is very rare ; but this has been well atoned for by "Jones," which, adding "John" again as a prænomen, would be (as has been well said by the Registrar-General) in Wales, a perpetual incognito, &c. (See the first page of this genealogy). Certainly "John Jones," in the Principality, is but a living contradiction to the purposes for which names and surnames came into existence.

DIRECT TAX OF 1798.

From the bound volumes of the Direct Tax of the State of Massachusetts, the original of which are in possession of the New England Historic Genealogical Society, of Boston, we make the following extracts relative to the Jones family :

JONATHAN JONES, owner and occupant of a house, of wood, in the town of Gerry, Mass., one story high, with eleven windows, fifty-four square feet of glass ; situated East on a town road, with an area of 960 square feet of land ; house and lot valued at 250 dollars. Also, one farm, west on Wm. Kendall, north on Ebenezer Tucker, East on a Pond, South on Thomas Legate, 130 acres, valued at 1690 dollars. One lot of Pasturage, plowing and mowing land, called Prescott Lot, 70 acres, valued at 840 dollars.

PRESCOTT JONES, owner and occupant of a house, of wood, East on County road, near the meeting-house, in Athol, area of square feet it covers, 444 ; 1 story high, 4 windows, 24 square feet of glass, and 40 acres of land, valued at 150 dollars. Land in Athol bought of Sylvanus Shirwin, near the meeting-house, 5 acres, with one barn, 31 by 20, shop 14 by 14, and an outhouse, all valued at 350 dollars ; one piece of land East and South by the road, North and West by Kimball Wood, 10 acres, at 100 dollars. One lot bought of Isaac Jones, 2 acres, 80 perches, valued at 20 dollars.

Amos Jones, owner and occupant, house and land in Athol, West on town road, North East corner of the town, area of square feet, 1008, house one story high, 11 windows, 47 square feet of glass, valuation of dwelling-house with lot, 260 dollars. One farm West on Silas and Ebenezer Chace, North on John Holman, East on Royalston line, 139 acres, 80 perches, with two barns, total valuation 1600 dollars. One meadow lot in Gerry, bought of Simeon Bruce, 3 acres, valued at 45 dollars. Amos Jones, a non-resident, owner of 70 acres of land in Royalston, valued at 250 dollars.

Isaac Jones, of Weston, one pasture in Gerry, West on Wind brook swamp, North on heirs of Benjamin White, 100 acres, valued at 800 dollars. A house in Weston, valued at 50 dollars ; and six lots of land, at 4923 dollars and 50 cents.

Benjamin Jones, of Templeton, 119 acres, at 1309 dollars ; one piece of pasturing in Gerry, west on Silas Sawyer, north and easterly on Templeton line.

Aaron Jones, Jr., Templeton, one house, 50 dollars. Two lots, 138 acres, valued at 1242 dollars, and 41 acres, at 200 dollars.

Lewis Jones, Royalston, 100 acres, valued at 300 dollars.

MANUSCRIPT OF NAHUM JONES, GERRY, JULY 1, 1806.

We now give some passages from the manuscript of Nahum Jones, the schoolmaster, before referred to (pages vii, 14, 18). Much of this is matter not incorporated in the genealogy. Commencing on page 15, he says : "The sons of Capt. Josiah Jones, jun. (eldest brother to my Great grandfather), were Josiah 3d, Daniel, William, and Elisha, active men " On page 15 of our book will be found a brief notice of " Capt. Josiah " and his children, with fac-similes of the signatures of the two Josiahs. The third Josiah of Mr. Nahum is of the fourth generation in our arrangement. Mr. Jones goes on to say,—" Josiah 3d removed from Weston to Stockbridge, in the County of Berkshire. Daniel removed to Lunenburgh. Elisha, the youngest, made a very active and enterprising man, was a man of talents and abilities, and well known throughout the State. He lived in Weston. He was a Colonel and Justice of the Peace. He had fourteen sons, and one daughter who was married to the late Rev. Asa Dunbar, of Salem. Col. Elisha Jones's sons were Nathan, Israel, Daniel, Elias, Ephraim, Elisha, jun., Josiah, Simeon, Stephen, Charles, Jonas ; the others died young. Col. Elisha Jones died in 1774 at an advanced age. His eldest son, Col. Nathan Jones, Esqr., was a man of great talents and very enterprising. He once purchased the town of Gouldsborough, in the District of Maine, part of which he sold to two merchants in Boston, Gould and Shaw. The town was named after Gould. Col. Nathan Jones removed from Weston to Gouldsborough, where he lived many years, and died a few months ago, aged 73. He greatly contributed towards the settlement of that country. He had the offer of being

Judge of the County Court, but did not accept. His brother Daniel had a college education at Cambridge; removed to Hinsdale, where he was made a Judge. He was a man of superior talents. He died a few years since. Israel is now living at Adams, in Berkshire County; has for many years been a Justice of the Peace and a member of the State Legislature. Josiah lives at Nova Scotia, and Ephraim in Canada. I am informed they are both Judges. Jonas lives in England, in affluent circumstances. Elias lives in Adams."

After this, Mr. Jones notices the sons of Capt. Nathaniel Jones, second brother of his great grandfather. Of these, Stephen and Ichabod are mentioned on pages 16 and 24 of this genealogy. In regard to Noah, brother to Stephen and Ichabod, he says on page 20, "Noah lived in Worcester; Col. Phinehas Jones, now living in Worcester, was his son."

"The sons of John Jones, senior, next brother to my great grandfather, James Jones, were Col. John Jones, Esq., of Dedham, Benjamin Jones, of Weston, Abraham Jones, of Weston, and Capt. Ezra Jones, of Barre. Ezra is still living. John and Benjamin died a few years ago, upwards of 80 years of age. Abraham was, perhaps, upwards of 60 when he died. Adam Jones, of Templeton, is Col. John's son, and Benjamin Jones, of Templeton, is Benjamin's son. Col. John Jones's son, Capt. John Jones, jun., was captain at the age of 30, in Canada, under Gen. Montgomery; died at the age of 32."

Col. John settled in that part of Dedham which is now in the town of Dover, Mass. He was born in Weston, Oct. 31, 1716; m. April 7, 1738, Anna Mixer, supposed to be the daughter of John and Abigail (Fiske) Mixer, of Watertown. Elijah Perry, Esq., of South Natick, a descendant of John Perry, of Roxbury, has a manuscript volume that came down to him from his maternal grandfather, this Col. John Jones, who was a Justice of the Peace. It is inscribed thus: "John Jones of Dedham, his book of Entery." The book is a common quarto, five quire blank, and contains the record of 380 cases, the trial, verdict, expenses, etc. In some instances three or four trial records are on a single page. Some specimens from these records were published in *The Norfolk County Gazette*, printed at Hyde Park, Feb. 2, 1878, and in the papers for the two following weeks. These extracts are interesting, and some of them, as matters of justice, quite amusing. Subsequently, two other articles appeared in the Gazette, one, an extract from another manuscript book, entitled,—"John Jones of Dedham's Book of Minits—In two parts, viz.: of the Danforths and some of their posterity to Jones's Family and Downwards, &c."

The other article gave some account of the life and home of John Jones, Esq. "A large number of his original sketches and plans are yet in possession of his grandson, Elijah Perry, Esq.," before mentioned. Justice Jones died February 2, 1802, at the age of 85 years, 3 months.

COLLATERAL CONNECTIONS OF THE LEWIS JONES FAMILY.

Had it entered into the plan of this work to trace out some of the collateral connections of this family, other than has been enumerated, it would have been a pleasing task. Much of this nature has been done by the indefatigable and erudite Dr. Bond, in his *History of Watertown*, pages 310 to 322 ; also on pages 814, 815, to which we refer all who are interested. We may briefly mention, however, that descendants of Lewis Jones are connected, by intermarriage, with Rev. Jeremiah Day, L.L.D., President of Yale College ; Col. Ephraim Williams, father of Col. Ephraim, the founder of Williams College ; Rev. Joseph Sergeant, missionary to the Stockbridge Indians ; Mark Hoppins, lawyer, of Great Barrington ; Hon. Theodore Sedgwick, father of the authoress, Miss Catharine M. Sedgwick ; Henry Williams Dwight, of Stockbridge, a member of Congress ; Rev. Enoch Thayer, of Ware, Mass. ; Rev. Stephen West, D.D., of Stockbridge ; Rev. Samuel Todd, of Adams, Mass., and others.

Ephraim Jones, born in 1750, son of Col. Elisha Jones, of Weston, settled in Canada. Two of his sons, Charles and Jonas, were members of Parliament, two of the daughters married lawyers, and one the High Sheriff of the District.

JOHNES OR JONES FAMILY, OF WALES.

While this genealogy was passing through the press, a pamphlet of 32 pages was received at the Library of the New England Historic-Genealogical Society, giving the lineage of a Welsh family, named Johnes or Jones. The book is in English, and entitled,—" Pedigree of the Ancient Family of [Johnes of] Dolau Cothi (now extinct in the male line), from the earliest period to the present time, compiled from various sources, by John Rowland, Welsh Secretary & Librarian to the late Sir Thomas Phillipps, of Middle Hill, Bart., F.R.S., F.S.A. Caermarthen, William Spurrell, 1877."

The last of the name was John Johnes, for many years Judge of the County Court of the District in Caermarthen, Recorder, &c., eldest son of John Johnes, High Sheriff for the county of Caermarthen, born in 1800. He was a descendant of Sir Thomas Jones, or Johnes. The original name was Ieuan or Ioan, corrupted into Jones. One of the Joneses of Llanfair, Clydogan, was the first called *Johnes.* The name is used variously ever afterward in the pedigree. The coat of arms is, in part, like that of Jones, Boultibrook, co. Hereford, bart. The motto is the same, *Deus pacit corvos* (God feeds the ravens). See page 2 of this work.

LEWES JONES, BISHOP OF KILLALOE, IRELAND (1633), AND HIS
SONS.

LEWES JONES was born in *Merionithshire* [North Wales], became a Student in this University [Oxford, England], in 1562 or thereabouts, but in what House I cannot tell. In 1569, being then Bach. of Arts, he was elected Fellow of *All-Souls* Coll. and about that time taking holy orders, went, without the taking of any other degree in this University, into *Ireland,* where he was made Dean of *Cashels,* and afterwards being nominated to the See of *Killaloe* in that Country, was consecrated thereunto on the 23d of *Apr.,* 1632. In 1641, when the Rebellion broke out there, and great Miseries followed thereupon, he retired to *Dublin,* where dying on the second of *November* in sixteen hundred forty and six, aged 104 years, was buried in the Church of St. *Werburgh,* commonly called St. *Warborough,* in the said city.

Wood's *Athenæ Oxonienses.* London, 1721, vol. II., column 1139.

Bliss, in his edition of the above work, printed in 1820, vol. IV., page 806, has this additional paragraph :

"Bishop Jones's son Henry was made bishop of Meath, 1661, and his son Ambrose, bishop of Kildare, 1667."

INDEX I.

JONES CHRISTIAN NAMES.

The figures before each name indicate the year of birth; those after, the page.

INDEX II.

NAMES OF PERSONS WHO HAVE MARRIED INTO THE JONES FAMILY.

The figures before the name denote the year in which the marriage occurred; the page is indicated by the figures after the names.

INDEX III.

NAMES OTHER THAN JONES.

The figures on the left show when the event occurred in connection with the name; on the right the page is given.

* The dates of publishment of these five females are on record. It is probable they married in the years mentioned, or soon after.

www.ingramcontent.com/pod-product-compliance
Lightning Source LLC
Chambersburg PA
CBHW031451270326
41930CB00007B/944